Rise To Your Best Life

From where you are to where you are to be

Elvis Prince Tognia

Printed in the United States of America

First Printing, 2014

ISBN 978-0-9908737-0-9

I dedicate this book, with great love, to my entire family. You not only gave me the opportunity to experience the gift of life but you are the reason I am inspired to inspire others.
For that, thank you.

CONTENTS

Introduction

I want you to know up front what this book is about, and how it came to be. My world completely changed when I discovered through voracious reading and significant research that within each of us exists a power so great that it has a potential to completely change the course of both our lives and the lives of others. To benefit from the effectiveness of this power, one must make a conscious and deliberate decision to tap into its vast potential. Only then, will you be able to rise from an ordinary to an extraordinary life.

This book is not a formula to live a wonderful life, nor to succeed at any undertaking, but rather it is a path of the transformation that I have come to discover and travel along which has given meaning and purpose to my life. My life has become one of endless possibilities, of purpose and happiness. The discovery and application of these principles have made it whole and complete. You don't have to take the lesson I am sharing here at face value. You have the absolute freedom to perform your own due diligence and to find whether this can work in your situation. I hope it will. Navigating through these findings, I literally felt like a "kid in the candy store". Saying that I was bewildered by this discovery would be the grossest of understatements. It was as though I had previously lived a life in complete darkness, in a way I had.

In fact, I was born in the city of Douala, in Cameroon. It is a country located slightly above the equator, in the center of Africa (the "armpit" of Africa; many would consider it to be in West Africa), with part of the South-west that is open to the Atlantic Ocean. But I grew up, for the most part, in the village of Tonga with my grandmother from the age of four simple because my parents could not afford to raise me in the city.

Life in the village could be stagnant, without much hope. Children go to school to "learn how to write their names". At least, this was what my grandmother used to say how important it was for me to go to school. Most children, after completing the primary school, went on to become farmers, like their parents and grandparents before them.

I had a tough childhood. We lived in constant lack, and what we suffered from most was hunger. I remember being truly hungry. And school wasn't easy at all for me, as I didn't always have supplies that could help me follow through. In our schools, students, parents for that matter were responsible for buying their own supplies, in all grade levels and of course for paying tuition. I was always borrowing things, from books to the simple ruler. One of the most physically challenging experiences was walking to and from school. To this day, I still remember as if it were yesterday the excruciating pain I felt on my toes, packed like sardines in the only pair of nylon shoes that I possessed for the entire school year. I walked approximately seven miles to school each day.

These sets of problems and hardship still haunted me, even after I had changed cities and schools. Before I attended the University of Douala, I might have changed schools more than six times. I did it for two reasons: It was to continue to the higher grade level that was not available in the village at that particular time, and also it was to find the cheapest school. In any city or school where I lived or attended at the given moment in time, it was as if I was carrying with me the germ of hardship. Even when I was attending college, it was still a real challenge for me to even study at night using a kerosene lamp. The feeble light emitted by the lamp could easily be detrimental to my vision - the eye problem that I experience today may have resulted from those moments. And I never lived in a house powered by electricity.

These life circumstances had conditioned me to have certain set of beliefs and thinking that were most damaging for my entire life. I thought that if you were born into certain conditions, you were destined to a resulting set of conditions. This thinking was reinforced by the saying that water flows into the rivers: it simply means in other terms that the rich becomes richer and the poor becomes poorer. To me, the line of divide was clear as day. That philosophy had led me to live in the darkness. I was like a condemned person in my mind. My discovery that we have the power to change the course of our lives was like a dense fog, evaporating under the powerful brilliance of a sunshine, a complete shift which in itself, was enlightening.

What I understood was that there are certain numbers of truths that pertain our lives. It is my experience that some principles naturally govern our lives, whether we are aware of them or not. These truths run their course, independent of our knowledge. Being aware of that reality, and using it to our own advantage, is the key to living a life of purpose, meaning and greatness; our best life.

I have spent a significant portion of my life, oblivious to this reality. Unfortunately, this is the case of people throughout the world who I have observed. These individuals may go through life, not having the slightest idea of what is going on around them, what they are really supposed to do, or what they are meant to be. I was living like a puppet. It was as though I was living someone else's life. And in a way, I was. I was going to school like everyone else. It seemed logical because that was what people did when they were young. Even the major I studied was someone else's idea. The beliefs and understandings of the things of life were that which prevailed in the community in which I belonged. I was far from imagining that things could be different. I thought that was all that there was about life.

I have to admit that coming to America has awaken my awareness to understand that it is up to each of us to lead the life that we set for ourselves. This understanding was made possible by the sense of freedom in many of its forms that this country defends and the innumerable resources that were available. What I have discovered through my experience and the experiences of many others that I have had the privilege to talk to or read from, is that there are certain approaches that can lift us from the plane of mundane to where things are true, simple, authentic, beautiful and permanent. This path can lead and guide us towards whatever destination we intend to travel. Whether you want to have a successful relationship, or a success in your career, in health, in finance and so on, adopting a better approach is exactly what makes a difference between people who live a dull life and those who live their best.

When you are poor, you believe a lack of money is the issue. Having grown up in the family where generation after generation suffered from harsh poverty, where the everyday struggle was to find what to eat, I picked up the belief that money could solve all of our problems. This seemed to prove pertinent, since it appeared that most of the problems we had were due to lack of money. The fact that among my siblings and me, I was the only one my family could afford to send to school, the fact that we lived in a run-down house that got flooded every single time it rained, even the fact that we never had electricity and every day was a struggle to eat, these, all seem to justify that belief.

But that belief was put into question after arriving in the USA over a decade ago. By then, I had seen and heard stories of people with money who have even more problems. There are people who seem to have decent jobs but are unhappy. For example, 90% of those working in the field of accounting that I encountered found their jobs boring and therefore were not happy. This challenged my belief and understanding. Back home, the title "expert accountant" was seen as an important and ideal job for many. I also have observed that this feeling of unhappiness is more manifest in the majority of people who start to develop anxiety by Sunday afternoon, going on Monday. Research shows that most cases of heart attack in the United States occur on Monday morning, between 8 AM and 9 AM when people are getting ready to go to jobs they don't like. In a similar vein, everyone, at least those who work Monday through Friday, seems to be happy on Friday because they are taking a weekend off from jobs they hate. In all honesty, this change of emotions doesn't happen when one does what they love and that was so much telling for me.

Even though I was still driven by the goal to earn money and help my family back home, in hindsight I realized a meaningful life was not simply conditioned by the pursuit of material wealth at least alone. Whether your life's goal is to obtain a financial freedom, career success, health or any other goal for that matter, there seems to be patterns that dictate success in any of these areas of life. Those patterns are a set of principles that work if you apply them. You must apply them in your life based on your situations and circumstances. People can help you, guide you, support you, but ultimately you are the one who decides to create change in your life. Nobody else can do it for you. Jim Rohn, a self-made millionaire and foremost American business philosopher once said that you cannot get someone to do your push-ups for you. You have to do them yourself to get the benefit. The same is true for these life principles.

In this book, you will find the path I took and some of the principles that I have come to embrace and have eagerly applied to myself in order to transform my life. I can assure you that I am completely a different person today than I was yesterday. And I guarantee that I will continue to become better tomorrow than today. Those who knew me growing up believe that there must have been a sort of mutation that occurred at some point in my life. Indeed, there has been. And that start of a transformation began when I discovered the principles that govern our lives, and started to apply them in my own life. My vision of the world had been altered. My life philosophy had changed. I replaced the old thinking and beliefs that had led me to where I was, with new ones that placed me at a different vantage point, one from which possibilities are endless, and from where I can see opportunities, abundance, peace and happiness.

Given my circumstances, the way I grew up and the thoughts that had governed my life in the past, I could not have been doing what I am doing today; becoming a speaker and empowering others to change their lives, just the way I changed mine. The path to live your best life that I mentioned in this book is the one I have come to know and have applied to be at this stage of the journey. It will help you see and understand that, it is indeed possible to become better in whatever area of your life you choose to improve. It is the principle of personal development that will take you from where you are to your best place in life

If, like me, you are establishing yourself in a new country(more precisely, in America), this book will help you to not only speed up your integration process, but also more importantly to help put you on the path towards a successful life.

If you have led a mundane life, this book will give you the perspective to ascend to a level of outstanding living. This is the undeniable truth: no matter where you are on the road of your life journey, no matter what your situation and your social position, by working on yourself and constantly improving your abilities, you will add more value to your stock. Only then you will become more valuable to your family, to your community, and most importantly, to the marketplace.

Now let's go -bon voyage!

Chapter 1

Developing an unshakable character

"You cannot dream yourself into a character: You must
hammer and forge yourself one"
— *Henri David Thoreau*

Character can best be understood as a mental and moral quality that an individual possesses.

It is what defines a person. That is to say, character is not something that we pick up from the society. We don't need the opinions of others to develop our own character. Even in total isolation, even in the barren desert or in the dense of the Amazon forests, we can continue to develop our character. It is like an onion that you peel, layer after layer, to reach to the core. It is like a sculpture that you chisel to find the perfect shape. Unlike the sculpture, character is an ongoing and dynamic lifelong process. Character has no final result, because every life situation or circumstance presents an opportunity to further evolve. A strong character allows us to persevere and find success when the times are tough and life truly difficult. Each of us has the opportunity to shape or build our own character, regardless of what challenges life presents to us. It is what we do in those most trying moments that makes us unique.

"Say no-even when you are hungry"

I have had the opportunity to mold the character that has led to be the person I am today. I grew up with my grandmother. I am not quite sure if I would have been different had my parents raised me, because I later learned that both my parents and my grandmother lived by the same life philosophy. We were many grandchildren - about nine of us in total - all, living with our grandmother in the three bedroom brick house. Our parents lived in the city of Douala and could not afford to raise us there. That was how we found ourselves cramped in with grandmother. She taught us a lesson that had shaped my life to this day: my grandmother told us, you "can always say no to any offer (food) even if you are starving."

Why would she advise us to resist any offer even if we had nothing else to eat?

In the village of Tonga where I grew up, the main occupation was subsistence farming. Almost every adult in the village possessed a farm; so did my grandmother. But the products from hers were not sufficient enough to feed us year-round until the next harvest season, simply because my grandmother was handicapped by an arm injury. Consequently, every year we experienced periods of severe starvation. We could easily go an entire week without food, often surviving on dry grains like corn and palm kernels. I can remember being really hungry.

But in Africa, villages are the places where traditions, rites, cults and even black magic are still alive and well.

Deaths are often associated with the practice of black magic. To avoid giving a reason to "enemies" to get to us so to speak, my grandmother formally instructed us never to take something offered by anyone in the village. We obeyed although it was the hardest thing we could possibly endure. It was even more difficult when someone with what were likely good intentions offered us something to eat. Imagine the difficulty, having to say "no, thank you" in times like this. It was often one of the most difficult things hungry children could bear. But perhaps it paid off, because in the end all nine of us were able to live till we left the village for the city, with no major incidents associated with witchcraft. We had escaped unscathed. This story seems rather bizarre, but it contains a lesson that is timeless for me.

The notion of "say no even if you are hungry" was the tool I used to chisel my character. It is not just the simple answer of saying "no," but rather living with the consequences of that no, facing challenges that come with, becoming tough and not giving up. How much hardship can we endure when we do have a choice? This is where many in life would choose the easy way out. It is not easy to pursue a dream when you can't pay your bills or have food on the table. It is not always easy anytime the going is tough. But at any moment of our existence we always have the choice to "say no even if we are hungry". In the school of persistence, it is said that when you don't give up, obviously you will reap the rewards. In my case, growing in the village and not giving in hunger, my reward was that I lived. I carried that lesson with me thorough my life.

I understood later in life that saying no does not apply

only when one is offered a hand out, but also to all things in life that call out our decision to choose. It could be, for example, an invitation by a friend to go shoot the pool or to hang out and play games. We have a difficult time saying no in these situations as well. The tendency is even more pronounced in teenagers, who are so often driven by the need to belong and to be accepted by their peers. It could be our boss who asks us to work over the weekend and finish up a specific project. There are so many demands in life that can impose on our time and effort. We sometimes say yes, believing that it benefits us to some extent. We often spontaneously say yes, even before we realize that we have other engagements, and then feel guilty that we may not be able to keep our word. Consequently it damages our relationship with others and the trust will vanish. Yet if we say no before saying yes, this approach can actually foster our relationship and build more trust.

The most important effect of saying no, however, is the ability to stay focused on what matters most in your life. You can only say yes to so many requests. Otherwise, before long, your own life will begin to crumble, and the loss will be entirely yours.

Saying no is never as easy as it seems, but we can always practice and remember to say no before we say yes. Know that when you say yes to something that is not important, you are in effect denying and saying no to something that is important.

Having come from a very poor family, it is a very intense internal fight between the need to carve my own life here in America and to help with every crisis that rises back home even though I know that if I don't financially intervene, it could sometime be fatal. I have to pick and choose when and how to intervene. There are many people who, like me, face the same dilemmas. This necessity to pick and choose should be applied to all other facts of life.

Saying no is rewarding, in so many different ways than saying yes.

We always have the freedom to choose

My grandmother's lesson also carried me through another difficult period of my life.

After I completed the first cycle of a secondary school, I had to continue the second cycle of a secondary school in a different village, called Bangangte. I was 13 years old, living for the first time by myself in a different village where I didn't know anyone. Not only did I have to pay my own tuition fees, I also had to provide for myself and my daily needs. I thought I had suffered starvation when I was with my grandmother, but this place added salt to injury. In fact, I only spent one year there, but it was a year that would be forever engraved in my brain. I literally almost died from hunger. The solution was as clear as day: to pack up my stuff and go back to the stay with my grandmother. Besides, who cared about school that would lead nowhere? After all, the goal for going to school was to learn how to write one's name; at least, that was my grandmother's definition of school. This was why about 95% of children in the village abandoned school, after completing one cycle of secondary school. Most went on to become farmers, like their parents and grandparents. I could have done exactly the same. I could have gone to help my grandmother with farming.

But I didn't. The meaning of my grandmother's lesson remained with me throughout those difficult moments. It even guided me. Though I spent most of my after school period lying in a semi-catatonic pose in bed, fatigued with hunger, I chose to go through the process

I realized that if I was to continue, I would need to create another reality, one in which I could survive. First I started to think that I must endure that situation, to be able to retell the story in the future. I thought it would make good storytelling for my kids. That idea became like dopamine, giving me the energy to finish what I had begun. I would need to find ways to have food, because that was my main problem. An idea came to me to talk to some villagers in my neighborhood about helping them in their farms on Saturdays and Sundays so I could get some potatoes or yams or plantains in return to bring home for my meals. That idea ultimately allowed me to endure and complete a school year.

The person I have become today is a direct result of the application of my grandmother's advice because at the underlining of the meaning of the lesson lies a notion of freedom of choice.

Where we are today is the results of the series of decisions we have made in the past, consciously or not. This signifies that in many life situations, we have complete freedom to control the outcome, by choosing what we think is best for us under the circumstances. This should be good news for us, because now we can start making different choices and decisions that would lead us to who and what we want to become in the future. The simple reality is that no matter what the choice, there is a price to pay, and of course, an eventual reward to reap.

Building a great character doesn't always mean having to brave adversity, but it is mostly what you become and what you do once you have overcome adversity. Although these challenges are uniquely what helps build a remarkable character, it should not mean that if you don't face challenges in life, you will not be a person of character. I personally know many individuals who are great examples to follow and role models for many, they didn't have to face obstacles or challenges to exude great character. Character is built from anything good or bad that may happen. Character is not something that you acquire and leave at that. It must be nurtured, just like a seed you plant under the ground that you must water, clear the weeds around them and make sure they have exposure to sunshine to get good nutrients from the soil and from the air. Character should be treated the same way; it is an active, artful endeavor. And it is a continuous process of a lifetime. Every day, we are presented with the opportunity to chisel away.

Courage is one element of a great character

After courageously braving any challenging situation, you must build upon it. I employ the word *courageously* because courage is one criteria of good character.

The Greek philosopher Aristotle once said, "A truly courageous person is not someone who never feels fear, but who fears the right thing, at the right time, in the right way." I want to explain what this really means by an opposite example: a person who engages in a reckless act of dangerous driving to the point of possibly losing his life, and the lives of others, would never be considered a courageous person; indeed, anyone who behaves as though they have nothing to lose would not be thought as courageous. A courageous act is a calculated one. I believe refusing a handout, even when the consequences of not accepting it were perilous was an act that resulted from great courage. At different moments of my life thus far, I have drawn upon this principle to guide myself through many situations.

When I started working on my dreams to help people to better their lives through motivational speaking and coaching, I became the laughing stock of my community. Those who knew me well thought I had lost my mind to have such a ludicrous dream, and I couldn't blame them. The standard path of life for many is to go to school and have a job and accumulate income for retirement. The ridicule, and possible shame, was apparent as family and friends labeled me as a selfish and overambitious type. But I had to courageously keep working the path that I had chosen for myself.

For me, the aspect of character that fashions me most is the sense of responsibility and the spirit of gratitude.

A sense of gratitude and responsibility

The dictionary defines gratitude as an attitude in acknowledgment of a benefit that one has received or will receive. One particular day in my very childhood, I found after coming back from school that there was nothing to eat. This often was the case. Fortunately, there were a few mango trees in our compound. During the period of arid harvest, mangoes often constituted our breakfast, lunch and dinner. I climbed up one of the trees and ate mangoes for my lunch: I was really famished. As if it were the first time, I began to notice all the fruit trees that were in the neighborhood and imagined that I would have starved to death if there were no mango trees. I thought that if I could eat all those delicious fruits, it meant that somebody had planted those trees. How generous were they to do that? I began to develop a feeling of appreciation for all things that I had the ability to enjoy in this life, to everyone who had had some impact in my life, however remote it may have been.

My idea of gratitude amplified when I came to the United States. I was amazed by the values this wonderful country defends. Most important was the concept of freedom, one that gives to citizens here the chance to become anything they so desire. It is a country that offers the opportunity to anyone to become the best one can become. It is a place where one's imagination can only be limited by the scope their own mind. Most importantly, it is where every citizen possesses an inalienable right "of life, liberty and the pursuit of happiness." How can one not be thankful of this "earthly eldorado"? It is very unfortunate that many who live here take these things for granted. When I give a talk, I always remind my audiences, especially the young ones, that one way to discover one's life purpose and have the drive to pursue something meaningful would be for them to see my native country, or any impoverish country in the world firsthand. They would come back a changed individual and would say "thank you" to this country.

The most common form of gratitude is the expression of thank-you. As humans, we have a natural tendency to express it when someone does us a favor or offers us something. We almost mechanically say thank you at times. This expression, so abused and discredited, has long since lost its rightful meaning. We say it, whenever and however. The simple attitude of gratitude demands that we appreciate what serves us in this life, whether it is a result of Mother Nature or human's action. When we really appreciate what we have around us, whether it be a result of human genius or the marvels of nature, we experience a palpable sense of liberation and relief. It is as though when we are grateful of all of these things, we are given like the permission to utilize all that we need for our existence. The law of attraction works best in this case. It is said that when you are thankful of what you have, the universe will arrange itself to bringing you more of the things that you are thankful for. This could not be truer.

When life provides us with all those wonders and beauties, we must take the responsibility not only to continue the flow of things, but also to contribute and to maintain that flow. When I acknowledged the creation left by others after that day I went up the mango tree, I felt a sense of indebtedness, perhaps not directly to those who planted the mango trees, but also to those who would come after me. I thought if others have sown the seed that I effortlessly harvest today, I must do the same for others to come; isn't it the law of life? In general we should be endowed with the feeling that we must do our part in this world. This sort of responsibility can be seen at the level of obligations or duty of a citizen. But great character doesn't result from simply doing what we are obligated to do, but rather from the things we do when we are not supervised. I think taking on the responsibility to add a positive impact in the world is thing of a great character.

Developing one is never complete. As long as we are alive, we must continue to shape and reshape our character at every step of our journey. This says every day we are given the opportunity to become better. There are questions that arise to this effect. Let's ask, for example, how tolerant or patient can you be in the face of a barrage of insults from a family member or friend who ridicules your decision to do something different? The answer: as much as we can be. It turns out that every situation is unique, requiring a unique way to approach it. Tolerance or patience is a virtue that can be cultivated, and those storming circumstances provide us a chance to do just that.

Chapter 2

We are born with unique talents and gifts

"The crowning fortune of a man is to be born to some

pursuit which finds him employment and happiness,

whether it be to make baskets, or broadswords, or canals,

or statues, or songs."

— *Ralph Waldo Emerson*

Life seems so miserable and empty when it is not supported by a definite purpose. You may have noticed that those who act as though they have nothing to lose do not have a convincing drive that gives them a sense of meaning. They don't have aspirations, dreams or purpose. They simply wander about life, responding to whatever life throws at them, rather than giving life a direction they want for themselves.

What is life purpose?

I think of purpose as life's mission, something that gives you a reason to live, to keep on keeping on when the going is tough and the future looks dismal. It is that force that is connected with you in the deepest level of your being. It is this one thing that arouses passion and enthusiasm to do what you love to do. Life is lifeless without it, and a person could live a risky and potentially dangerous life. It is truly sad to realize that the majority of people go through life without discovering their life's purpose, much less knowing that such a thing even exists. The direct consequence is that they end up being part of other people's agenda. The illustration of that assessment can be seen within the employment spectrum- not that there is anything wrong with being employed. But my point here is to show that we are employed sometimes to be part of the accomplishment of someone else's dreams. It is easy to spot the lack of purpose in one's life by the way he/she carries oneself, their attitude, their energy and their way of life in general. I sincerely believe that there is a correlation between happiness and life purpose. There seems to be a moment of magic when one realizes why they are here on earth and what they have been called upon to do.

Once I discovered what my purpose was, my life shifted dramatically. It was as though I had born anew. I became almost a different person. My definition of happiness changed, as well.

Once we believe in our core being that we are here on earth for a reason, it is quite an enlightened realization. It becomes even more magical when we discover what that reason is.

I used to belong in the masses of those who never figured out their calling, wandering about and wondering in awe what had just happened in life. I was simply following the bandwagon and most of the time fell into the agenda of other people. It is unfortunate to lead such a life of complete desperation.

Back in Cameroon, the major I chose in school was not a well-thought out idea: it was simply what all of my closest friends were choosing. The circumstances were completely different, and so this was somewhat justifiable. A country where unemployment was past fifty percent, where its population lived under the poverty line(even by the standards of an underdeveloped country), there was really not much of a choice other than fighting for survival. People only do what they have the privilege to be offered as long it puts food on the table.

But what I couldn't understand was the fact that after arriving in the United States, I witnessed a sort of massive convergence of my fellow compatriots into specific types of job. I simply found it odd that nearly everyone I knew at that time was going to school to become a nurse or obtaining a quick certification to be nurse assistant. I thought that this was America where there were endless possibilities. There couldn't possibly be just one important type of career field. I was even advised (with good intentions) by friends and family members that I must be a fool not to do nursing, that there are so many job offers in that field. With the Baby Boomer generation getting older, it was understandable that the market would expand for these types of career field. But in all sincerity, not everyone was born to become a nurse or any other existing profession. I politely declined their offer of good intention, and instead began to ask myself other questions; such as what are other possible career fields out there? How can I go about to pursue them? While the questions were brewing inside of me, I began working at the grocery store and taking some English classes. Later, I enrolled in some college courses, while remaining undecided as to the major. As time flew by, my questions were no longer centered on what was possible out there, but rather on what was possible for me. I turned inward. What were my strengths or qualities? I began to look on the inside, rather than the outside. By then, I was developing a knack as a "go-to-guy" at the grocery store. I became that guy with the accent who always made customers feel good. In fact, in that store, the manager did something that had never been done in the history of that company. He instructed the store artist to make a poster of me with my natural smile. I am not sure exactly when they did it, but one morning I was coming to work as usual, when lo and behold, a big poster of me was looking back at me, displayed all over the store. On it was written "happiness is contagious." Customers would ask copies for their homes, cars and offices. I have to admit, it was really a nice touch and I was so ecstatic about it. Then it dawned on me: I reasoned, if people were happy that I was happy, I might indeed possess a gift that could impact people's lives. Herein, began the idea of my life's purpose, to empower people with my smile. Frankly, after the moment of fame had waned, I sort of forgot about that idea of helping people, as I was still under pressure of the things of life. Besides, I didn't have any knowledge as to how to go about doing such things, or to possibly make a living off of it. But it was only years later that I was able to pick it up and reconsidered the possibility of making it an objective to attain.

Only a handful people that I know seem to love what

they do. According to many surveys, around 80% of people in North America don't like their jobs. It is evident that those who don't know their passion in life, simply stick with whatever is available for them. There is also a number of people who believe that their passion can never help them pay the bills or survive.

How to discover one's passion

Only few years ago, I could not have defined what I wanted to do for the rest of my life. I was going from job to job, hoping for the miracle of life. I was driven only by how much a particular job would pay and what was available. When I look back now, I can't help but realize how uncertain and random life was. The question of life's purpose seems out place for many people, and this is very unfortunate. I was truly surprised to observe that in a country like the United States, lots of people do not have a clue as to what their passion really is. You would think it is understandable in poor countries, where food is one of the rarest commodities, that one would not think about passion. The reason is simply that the economy is weak, there are no jobs and even the few jobs available are reserved for the undeserving number of people who get there as a result of a broken and corrupted system. The majority live in a constant fight for survival. Therefore people's "passion", if one exists, is a quest for food. People's consuming and predominant thought is to find a sustainable source for their daily bread. They think less of anything else. There is a saying in my culture that the "hungry belly has no ears." It simply means that when we are hungry, we can't focus on anything. Even when people may have the slightest idea of their passion, they would bury it as quickly as it appears or simply contemplate it as a mere fantasy. The socio-political and economic system of the country is not fertile ground to creatively work on the passion and thrive.

But in a country like the United States, where I have reason to believe that food is not the main concern, many people remain clueless as to what they are here on earth for.

First, I believe in the "things happen a reason" saying. I believe that I am here in this world for a specific reason, as is everyone else. We were chosen out of millions of sperm cells to accomplish a specific task. Each one of us is unique. We possess greatness within ourselves. We all have talent in one area or another. Some people have the serendipity to tumble into what really matters about their lives. They know from a very young age what really appeals to them, what fascinates them and they waste no time to put their talents into use. This is the case of those who, at a relatively young age, have already accomplished incredible feats and attained a level of success nothing short of outstanding. The wealth that they accumulate often surpasses the budget of some countries. Society, and especially the media, make their ratings often, by flushing them out and covering extensively about their lives. Recent examples in the entertainment and media industry include the likes of Justin Bieber, Taylor Swift, and Mark Zuckerberg to name a few. They discovered their talent early on, and devoted themselves to working toward it realization.

There is no one way and no one formula to actually discover one's passion. But it is important to adopt the right approach. I often advise my clients and invite my audience to go back in time, to explore what once held their attention when they were children, and to ponder on the matter. It could provide clues as to where their true passion might lie.

Asking the right question is a way to achieve clarity regarding life's purpose. A question such as "Who am I" and "What am I on this earth for?" elicit a response that is purpose driven. It really doesn't matter how the question is formulated, but when that question is uttered, it is like a request sent to the universe. Your subconscious mind picks it up and goes to work to deliver the right answer to you. This process of expressing a thought to the infinite power of the subconscious mind respects the law of life described by Joseph Murphy in his well acclaimed book **The Power of Your Subconscious Mind**. The answer often comes in the form of an idea called a hunch that pops up in your head, or the answer comes in the form of a dream. That is why it is important to pay attention to ideas that come to us during waking reality and to those that appear in our dreams. When dealing with these topics, you must remain alert and aware and have an open mind to receive what is rightfully destined. In general, those who have an open and even inquisitive mind gain more new insights and development than those who refute anything that even remotely challenges their beliefs. Sometimes, you might develop ideas from what you read, see or hear. A conversation might illicit such an idea. A seminar, a video, even traveling can prompt an insight.

We must understand that dreams are not merely a series of uncoordinated, distorted and meaningfulness images visiting our unconscious mind when we are not awake. In fact, according to Gillian Holloway in **5 Steps to Decode Your Dreams**, dreams are our key to solving many issues of our lives. Our dream can be a clue to what is going on in our lives and uncovering our dream can be the answer to the question of our passion.

Another way of tapping into your potential can be by using simple logic as follow:

Make three circles or three lists.

In the first circle write everything that you love to do.

In the second circle, write all that you are good at doing.

In the third circle, write everything that is meaningful to you.

In the overlapped area of the three circles exists what could be considered your passion.

With the lists, do the same as you did with the circles except keep the lists separate. The items that appear in the three lists are what you could to bet on to be your passion.

In the end it is about what really drives you, what moves you. It is about that one thing that brings you fulfillment.

Sometimes, your dream can be pieced together from small and often remote loose-end ideas. But again you have to connect the dots so that things can easily fall in place.

In the very strange way, when I was coming to the United States, I had this silly thought that I would tell African stories to Americans. I imagined that people would be curious about me, my life and my past and I would readily tell them my story.

When I arrived, I had as a mission and personal responsibility to help my family and the village at large. So, helping others was my mission.

And once I was here, I somehow fell in love with the stage. I've done a few things on stage such as dance performances on television, and I have performed at colleges.

It all falls in place to realize that being a motivational speaker allows me to be on stage helping other people to change their lives by telling them my story.

Many people never work on their passion

It is sad to know that many people know full well their life purpose, and yet they deny themselves to help others' dreams come true. This reality can be evidenced by the fact that more people in Northern America don't like what they do. The common response they provide as to why they don't work on their dreams is that they don't know how to make a living from it. Others would argue that they strive for security and try to persuade you that, "You don't play around when you have children." This rhetoric is my friend's excuse not to work on her dreams. Some would even say that the field of their passion is pretty much saturated, or it doesn't pay. A friend told me once that I should be realistic and that, "Africans don't dream when they come to this country (America)." Unfortunately, that is exactly the opinion of many of my fellow Africans who come here. This can be illustrated by the fact that many of them and some other immigrant groups cluster in a specific type of job or career field - I have no problem with a particular field; in fact, I love some of them. They are noble jobs and of service to others. In the few cities of the United

States that I visited, I have observed that a particular immigrant group from the Middle East dominated city taxi cab drivers. Also, Filipinos leaned toward the nursing field. The trend applies to many other immigrant groups.

It saddens me to see people with great and rare talents sacrificing themselves on jobs that don't help them grow. This is one of the reasons I created a coaching program to help immigrants like me find their niche in this country where possibilities are endless.

The solution to working on the dream is quite simple: You can work full time on your job and part time on your dream because you can always have enough time to do anything if you want it badly enough.

We are caught up with life's distractions and with the advancement of technology today, we are being disconnected from life's essentials. We can't seem to concentrate any longer on the things that matter the most. And we claim to lack time for anything other than what we busy ourselves with. Doesn't it make you mad that those who are successful have the same number of hours in the day? But it is what they do during those hours that makes all the difference. They work on their dreams. We are spending more and more hours a day in entertainment. In fact, a new study by a researcher at the San Diego Supercomputer Center (SDSC) at the University of California, San Diego, says that by 2015, the sum of media asked for and delivered to consumers on mobile devices and to their homes will take more than 15 hours a day to see or hear. That almost equals our waking life, and it is spent on things that don't matter. If we calculate how much time it amounts to in a month or a year, it almost equals one's entire lifetime. Imagine if only a portion of that time were used to work on something that is meaningful. Soon enough the dream will come to life. We can suppose another possibility; we have 24 hours in a day. If we spend 8 hour on sleep and 8 on work, that leaves 8 hours. If we could use just 1 hour every day to read, to learn a new skill, to learn a new language, to listen to a motivational audio tape or video, to invest on ourselves, to work on the object of our passion, soon it will start to matter. We will be amazed at where it will lead us a few years. Whether the object of your passion requires more education or a different job, you can find time to work on it. Simple discipline and plan of action are required.

When I knew what I wanted to do for the rest of my life, I immediately went to work on what was required for me do what I love. When I came to the US, I learned just enough English to get by and to be understood. And I was having a hard time fitting in and conversation was difficult. But when it was clear to me that public speaking was my passion, I started to read almost every day. I knew reading would improve my vocabulary which I need to clearly communicate my message and to understand the world around me. I also needed to learn more about my field. So reading for me was one of the most important things to do to give myself a chance at the public speaking business. I read every chance I got. Rather than eating or dozing off during my lunch break, I read. I sat up to read at least 30 minutes every night. Honestly, I may have skipped a few days, but I have maintained consistency. Being a non-English speaker, I had a disadvantage to other aspiring speakers who were native English speakers. I knew I had to work twice as hard to reach their level and even harder if I wanted to be better than they were. The amazing thing about working on your dream is that it doesn't feel like a job that you are obliged to do. Once you conceive in your mind and believe in your heart that something is the one thing for you, every ounce of your being is attuned to its realization. The process becomes fun.

The secret of great living is doing what you love. It brings happiness and emotional well-being. It is a key to success. Many people who have achieved outstanding results and great success have done what they love most and they don't hold back from emphasizing it. (Steve Jobs Stanford commencement address in 2005). You don't find hardship in working on your passion. Sometimes the line that separates work from fun is blurred and you often look forward to going to work on your dream.

Unfortunately, as Henri David Thoreau says, "Most men lead lives of quiet desperation... and go to the grave with the song still in them." The majority of people take their dreams to their graves. No wonder someone said that the richest place on earth is not the gold and diamond mines in Africa, but the graveyard. There, you will find dreams that have never been realized, talents that have never been discovered, and many other natural gifts that have never been shared. What a pity!

There is another important humanitarian benefit in pursuing your dreams. In doing so you are contributing to the greater good in this world. The bee has a goal of seeking nectar. It has no intention of going beyond that. But in the process, it affects the continuity of human life and vegetation by cross-pollination. When we pursue our dream, no matter what it is, we are setting an example for other people and making a positive impact in the world.

In pursuing a speaking career, it is my hope that many immigrants who come to the USA, specifically those with a different language of origin than English, will find it possible to help others by telling their stories. I believe we all have stories to tell than can inspire someone else's life. If we all pursue our dreams, this path may lead us to a better world.

Chapter 3

Create a plan of action and work your plan

"The vision must be followed by the venture. It is not enough to stare up the steps- We must step up the stairs."
— *Vance Havner*

It is absolutely necessary to identify something that you are passionate about. This is the starting point of all realization; it is not enough. The simple wish must be supported by a plan of action to make it become reality. Any passion should be nourished and even protected against an attack from all fronts notably negative self-talk and negative outside attacks. Any purpose, when backed by a plan of action plus persistence will come to pass. Persistence is the key to the accomplishment of any dream. When you start on your dream no matter what the nature or the size, it is highly likely that you will encounter moments of turbulence; you will face challenges and obstacles. What gets you through is determined simply by how hungry you are. If you are not hungry enough, you will give up and quit and that will qualify as failure. That will be the end of the road for you and you will only recall it as once upon a time when you had a dream.

But if you persist no matter what obstacles you are facing, if you make a mental, deliberate decision that you will continue until you see it take shape, then your dream will come to pass.

Many people don't have the luxury to enjoy the final product of persistence because they can't afford to push a bit harder, stay just a bit longer. They quit only "Three Feet from the Gold."

The fable of "Three Feet from the Gold" illustrates the story of a man who had discovered a vein of Gold. He acquired all the equipment necessary and started digging. After a period of fruitful effort that was about enough to compensate the cost of the equipment, the vein of Gold disappeared. He got frustrated, quit and abandoned the mine. It was later discovered by someone else that the vein of Gold picked up only three feet from where the man had stopped digging.

This analogy told by Napoleon Hill in **Think and Grow Rich** is simply the application of the lesson of persistence and perseverance.

When you set your plan and work your plan with the idea of persistence in mind, it is highly likely that you will accomplish your desire.

The action plan is likened to a map that will guide you to your destination. Just imagine that you are going to a specific destination and you don't have a map. It is likely that you will find yourself far away from your destination. It is the same as working hard to climb the ladder of success only to find out that it is leaning against the wrong wall. You must create the map that will guide you to the right destination.

In most cases the type of plan of action or the formulation of the different steps to follow results inherently from the desired goal. For example, if your desire is to become a teacher, it is fitting to understand that it entails going to school and obtaining the necessary degrees and credentials; you must submit an application to the desired school. It is pretty straightforward.

But sometimes the accomplishment of the object of your desire may require a bit of creativity for its plan of action. There is no known or established route as in the case of becoming a teacher. Most artists appeal to the power of creative imagination to arrive at the finished product of their artistry.

But many people fail to tap into and engage this part of themselves: the infinite intelligence of the creative imagination. It is proven by science that we only use a fraction of the mind's potential. Those who dare to delve more in this oceanic expanse often arrive at outstanding discoveries. Many are called genii. History has recorded a number of individuals who employed methods such as meditation, prayer and the principle of auto suggestion to come up with ideas and formulas that were life innovative. Such individuals are Leonardo De Vinci, Michelangelo, Einstein, Johann Von Goethe Wolfgang and many more.

We too can utilize some of those methods to figure out how to concretize what we love. Those who claim that they could never make a living from what they love think that way because there is no known path for the realization of their desire. Some people create an opportunity when they don't see one available. This principle has seen a boom in its application in our society today with the advent of technology where people are creating at record pace solutions to fulfill certain societal needs. Such is the creation of different applications and all sorts of media connective platforms such as Facebook, Twitter, Linked In and numerous Apps.

You simply must think creatively to put in place the strategies necessary to arrive at the desired destination.

One of my clients was working at a retail store, but he had a passion for fitness and overall wellness. He worked out at least five days a week and he was particular about his nutrition. He also gave advice to others when asked since his physique would allow him to compete for bodybuilding if he were so inclined. It didn't enter his mind that he could become a personal trainer until I mentioned that to him. Even at that point he was somewhat reluctant to consider the possibility because he had grown comfortable at his job, having been there for more than a decade. Eventually he came up with a plan not only to start working as a fitness instructor for kids during summer, but to create videos to reach many at once. His ultimate goal is to own a fitness center.

This is simply to say that no matter what is the passion, there are ways to live from what you love and to thrive. If you love sports, for example, there is a myriad of ways to thrive at what you are passionate about. You can play a sport, coach a team, write a sport column in the newspaper, work in team management; you can become a broadcaster or sport commentator. If you organize your life around what you truly love, it will be easier to make a living from it.

Most of the time you don't need to see the whole picture to start working on your dream. It is in doing something that the whole picture will start to take shape. You don't even need to see the whole path in front of you to start the journey. It is like driving from one place to another at night or in the fog; with the headlights you can only see a few yards ahead. As you advance, the road will become clear, so it is with your journey to realize the object of your desire. It is a fantasy to think that everything must be clear or perfect for you to start working on your dream. The road that leads to success is not a straight line, but rather a swirling, curving and bumpy road with sometimes divergent similar other roads that delude you. But you have to be on the road to hope to arrive at your destination.

Unfortunately, many people are not so adept at the principle of _ stick ability_ that says you have to stick to it until you see the outcome, until the result is possible.

Many of us are wired to want it now: Instant gratification

Often, succeeding in doing what you love requires a good degree of effort and time.

There is no such thing as overnight success. Even though it is common in our society to believe that there are some lucky people who, as a result of being in the right place at the right time become successful. But if we listen to their stories, we will find that what we consider an overnight success is indeed the result of many years of intense preparation. The example of the supposed overnight successes can be seen in show business where an actor or a singer becomes a blockbuster personality. Some people thought how lucky Jennifer Hudson was when she became sensational after the movie, *Dreamgirls*. Although it is the movie that lifted her to the pedestal of Hollywood fame, some people didn't know that she had been singing since she was little and she was a runner up in the third season of American Idol. Or Lupita Nyong'o, who won the Academy Award for best actress for the supporting role in *12 Years a Slave*. Many do not know that she has studied film and theater in London and New York and has starred in numerous films in Kenya. Overnight success is rare. Maybe the lottery winners are an exception. They could be considered overnight successes. But usually these types of success don't last and cannot be really classified as true success.

Success can be defined as a steady progress towards one's goals. Winning the lottery is simply the fact of chance. Studies show that lottery winners return to the level of happiness they had before winning the lottery after about 6 months and most of them become broke in less than 10 years. Don't be fooled by the small rewards of today.

The idea of wanting something now can be traced back in the era of hunter-gatherers when our ancestors had to stay alert, as the toothy tigers were also out hunting. And, unfortunately, human beings were among its prey. The hunters had to scan for danger and whatever was needed for the family was needed now because tomorrow was uncertain. Today, the concepts of competition, technological challenges and disease have amplified this idea of wanting things to happen yesterday. In our society it is important for us to get a lot done, but at the same time, we want it now. Obtaining something immediately doesn't guarantee a long-lasting effect.

I have found this topic particularly interesting in many immigrant communities where many get fooled by the overwhelming possibilities of job opportunities. The United States is one of few countries with low unemployment rate. For many who come from countries where jobs are as scarce as gold, and I say this from experience, we get very pleased and excited that anybody can work here. Consequently, we plunge ourselves in whatever job shows up first because of the need to pay rent, buy groceries, clothing and pay other bills. Especially upon our arrival we don't have much choice about jobs because we don't speak the language or have the experience, and we feel it is necessary to start somewhere. Before we know it, we get stuck in a job. Two things happen. First, we cannot leave because we have to pay the bills. It seems dangerous to lose that job. Second, we get comfortable with our job. Don't we often hear people say, "as long as it pays the bills," they have no problems. Sometimes people trade one job for another with only a slight difference in the dollar amount per hour. In any case, this perceived obligation to gain *now* stifles our ability to creatively think about our passion and to work persistently and consistently to reach our dreams.

Good things come to those who wait: Delay gratification

Between 1960 and 1970, a series of studies was led by psychologist Walter Mischel, then a professor at Stanford

University. The objective of the studies was to analyze the impact on children of delaying gratification in terms of their future success. In the studies, 4 -year- old children were placed in a room with a marshmallow in front each of them. They were told that the marshmallows were theirs to eat. They were left by themselves for approximately 15 minutes, after which the experimenter returned and those who had resisted eating their marshmallows were given an additional one. After the instructor had left the room, there were theatrical movements in the room with children finding ways to resist eating the marshmallows. One child hid under the table as to avoid seeing the treat. Others would walk away from it; even others would sniff the delectable candy and so on. In the end some children couldn't resist. Others held their impulses and got their just reward upon the instructor's return. The follow-up studies many decades later proved that the children who resisted eating the marshmallows were doing well academically and surpassing those who gave in by 200 points in SAT's scores. They had better life outcomes.

This experiment illustrates the application of the principle of success in life. Short cuts and quick fixes will never lead to a permanent, sustainable success. Success demands avoiding the low road and being persistent. Many of us fall short of accomplishing our desires because of the child in us. Many of us can't resist eating the marshmallows. We all want reward but are unwilling to brave the challenges and put in the time necessary. I have noticed this need of reward without effort in my three-year-old daughter. She likes braided hair; she shows off at school and enjoys the attention she receives for her braids.

She enjoys looking in mirror, but she is unwilling to sit down so that her mom can perform the exhausting task. The braiding can take hours to complete; she is not willing to pay the price.

As adults, we act the same way. We are crippled by the fear of failure and fear of the unknown.

During my workshops, some attendees entertain the idea of becoming successful at a particular profession but when they learn how many years are required, they are bewildered and believe that they cannot wait long. They fail to see that whether it is 5 years, 10 years or even 20 years, time will pass regardless of what they do or don't. By not acting, one can remain in the same spot for 20 years. Napoleon Hill spent more than 20 years working on discovering and taking to the world the principles of success before he actually became successful.

The Chinese proverb "A journey of a thousand miles begins with a single step" is not just rhetoric, but rather a practical application of an action plan, because when you start a journey, the incontestable truth is that you will arrive at a destination one day.

We must go through the process. So it is almost impossible to decide on a new direction for your life today and become successful tomorrow. If success were that easy, everybody would be successful. Unfortunately, a small number of people appear to have and enjoy so much while a large number tend to fight over little and wonder how life can be unfair. You must put in the time required until you arrive at the destination. What distinguishes the few from the majority is not that they were born with unique abilities. In fact, we all have something special within us, but some work on their passion almost all the time and they enjoy doing it even if the reward seems far away. To do so requires a plan of action and discipline; you have to put in the time working on your dream and do it consistently. Make sure that the activities accomplished day by day are in congruence with your desired outcome. Normally, when you determine the object of your desire, you should be automatically engaged to start working on it because it contains within itself the motivation factor. But there are still moments when one may not be completely convinced and still find it difficult to find time to work on the passion. I believe there is always time for anything.

Malcolm Gladwell in his book, **Outlier; The Story of Success**, came up with proof that one must put in 10,000 hours of practice to be the expert in a specific field. Ten thousand seems a lot of hours some people would say. But how many hours do they spend on things that don't matter. Just do it. Start by spending the first hour in the practice of your field. Nine thousand nine hundred ninety nine hours remain. Maybe that approach will help. This notion of 10,000s simply means that the more you practice, the better you will be. Better yet you will become an expert when you reach a certain number of hours working in your field. You can't be in a hurry and you can find time to do it.

Once I became convinced that helping people achieve great result in their lives was what I was born to do, it was as though time made itself available for me, my schedule got rearranged so that I could work on my dream. I did so by eliminating the unnecessary activities such as television, internet surfing and other media moments that were taking up my time. I cut out unnecessary phone conversations.

I am the father of four beautiful kids, and I was working full time on a job where I barely made ends meet; debt piled up every month. I had to be very creative as to where I could find time to work on myself and on my passion for being a speaker. I had to sacrifice my lunch time to read. Every moment I spent driving was an opportunity to learn. I had and I still have a lot of books on tape so I listen while driving. I now look forward to driving long distances, and I enjoy the moments. It doesn't matter to me when there is the bumper-to-bumper traffic typical in a city like Los Angeles in certain hours. I have read in an article that two years of driving in a city like Los Angeles is equivalent to the time for acquiring an academic degree, and I cannot agree more. At home I listen to educational videos while cleaning the floor or doing other household tasks. One of my favorite pastimes is washing dirty dishes. We use lots of dishes because we always cook at home; therefore I clean them twice or three times per day. Something magical almost always happens at the kitchen sink. For me it is a place and moment for thinking. My mind runs efficiently at that time. Great ideas come to me while I am doing the dishes. The kitchen sink is a meditation spot. The clinking of the plates or the running of water is mind stimulating. Speaking of the running of water, taking a shower is another moment of intense reflection for me as well. I believe finding a moment to think is critical to the process of working on your dream and reflecting on your life. Any of these small activities are not meant to change the course of my history. It is a simple plan in action toward a goal that I set for myself, a goal that is remote. You don't have to do the dishes or follow any of my steps to accomplish your own goals. Set your plan of action based on your circumstance and what is available to you. The general idea is to find what works for you, and just do it.

I believe that if you want something badly enough, you will find time to do it. There is this popular story of a young man who asked a guru what is the secret of success. The guru said to him that if he really wanted to know the secret of success, he must meet with him early in the morning at the beach. When the young man got there on time, the guru was already in place, but half immersed in the water. When the young man approached him in the water, the guru grabbed him and pushed his head under the water. When he was about to pass out, the guru pulled him out and asked him what he wanted the most when his head was under the water. He said he needed air, he needed to breathe. At that moment nothing mattered, not parties, not television, not friends, nothing. So the guru said, "When you get to the point that you want to succeed as badly as you want to breathe, then you will succeed". This story is not a mere metaphorical tale of success, but the example shows the strong power of the desire to succeed. When you think and believe that your life makes sense if and only if you accomplish what your heart desires, when you work on your dream as if your life depends on it, then you will have the desire to succeed.

History shows that those who find their passion the only thing that matters have devoted every ounce of their being to succeed. This is to say whatever it is that you are pursuing, if you put in the necessary time and effort, you will succeed. Understand that success here is simply a steady progress toward your goals, the goals you set for yourself. Persistence is of key importance at this stage of the success journey. You can't expect to set your goals today and accomplish them tomorrow.

The principle of Goal setting

Goal setting is the strategy that you employ to establish a plan of action and to measure progress. The objective is to arrive at the accomplishment of your desire faster. The goal is the direction you want to take to arrive somewhere.

The first thing to do is to ask a question about what you want. You could phrase it this way, "What do I want in life?" The question will illicit an answer that is purpose driven. You will form a big picture of what you want and when you want to achieve it. A big goal could take years to accomplish.

So you can set out to achieve it in 5, 10 years or more.

Then, break the big picture into smaller goals or steps. It is looking at the different stages that will lead to the big picture. These different steps should have their own time frame.

You could also set mini goals and accomplish them daily, weekly or monthly. At this level, the daily to-do-list is most important because it is the detail of the action plan.

Let's take an example with simple calculation. If your big picture is to accumulate one million dollars in 5 years you can break it down as follow:

In two years you must have $400,000.

In 6 months you should have $100.000.

In a month you should have more than $16000.

Every day you should be putting aside close to $600.

That gives you an idea of what you have to do daily.

Another aspect of goal setting is to celebrate every leg of achievement to keep the momentum going.

So it takes time to accomplish a major goal. But it is important to notice and measure improvement or progress toward the goal. Otherwise, we can be easily fooled doing over and over the same thing that doesn't work without realizing that we have not budged from the point of departure. You have to measure progress; you have to see if the activities you are doing today are taking you toward where you want to go.

Kaizen

Another way of keeping track of progress is actually employing the method of Kaizen.

Kaizen refers to the philosophy or practice that consists of continuously improving. It is a Japanese term and was first used by businesses after the Second World War. The use of Kaizen helped rapidly reconstruct the Japanese economy after the disastrous war and the annihilation of Nagasaki and Hiroshima. Since then, this philosophy of continuous improvement has been used on any area where the need of change or improvement was required. A way to measure progress is by deciding that one percent is all you need every day. It is the small improvement every day that will lead you to where you want to go. Don't miss a chance to add only one percent wherever you are on your journey. The reason to apply this method is simply because small improvement may not be noticed and failure to notice progress can cause discouragement. By applying the method regardless of how visible the improvement can be, you are adding value to your stock. Little by little everything will start taking shape in your life. When I learned about this Kaizen method, I made sure no two days of my life remained the same in terms of improving myself and my abilities. No matter how busy I was with other things in life, I always tried to improve everyday however small the improvement might seem. The perfect example was when I set up a health goal with the exercise regime. When I started working out, I could do only one pull-up, four crunches and seven push-ups. I decided I was going to use the Kaizen. Then I would always add something to what I was already doing. For example, I would do one more repetition, one more set, one more minute and it was the same with any other exercises. In the end, I was able to accomplish 30 pull-ups in one set and 50 push-ups in one set. The idea of improving was working. Workout is the perfect example to start cultivating this discipline of continuous improvement. I mention workout because it is wise to consider the health goal part of whatever goals one sets. When that discipline is well ingrained, it will affect any other goal through osmosis. In life everything affects everything.

The 80/20 rule

When establishing a plan of action, you must take in consideration the 80/20 rule.

The 80/20 rule also called the Pareto rule is a principle that, when applied will increase productivity and focus. The principle was originally invented by Wilfredo Pareto, the Italian economist who discovered in 1906 that 20 percent of the population in Italy owned 80 percent of the land. He observed the same reality with pea pods in his garden where 20 percent of pea pods produce 80 percent of the peas. Businesses use this principle to boast about their productivity by identifying the 20 percent of key elements and activities that produce 80 percent of the result. Businesses concentrate on the 20 percent.

No matter what you are pursuing, you can apply this principle to increase your effectiveness and quickly bring about the result. You must identify those key activities that generate the majority of outcome and concentrate on them. This principle calls for the principle of prioritization which is about keeping the main thing main. The application of the 80/20 principle helps avoid being impeded by the busyness of life. Many people claim to be busy. They are busy without being productive.

This idea of being busy is commonplace in America. Everybody seems busy and looks busy. As children grow into adults, they pick up this social habit and they become busy individuals. The application of this 80/20 principle helps us filter out clutter and concentrate on what matters.

You can apply this principle to any situation in life, whether you want to lose weight or make sales. You are going to realize that about 20 percent of your activities produce the result.

Generally, in sales for example, you can observe that 20 percent of salespersons bring 80 percent of sales.

Chapter 4

Think healthy

"When health is absent, wisdom cannot reveal itself, art cannot manifest, strength cannot fight, wealth becomes useless, and intelligence cannot be applied."
— *Herophilus*

As we go through life doing what we do and pursuing our dreams, we tend to forget to take care of ourselves. We ignore the important thing that allows for our very existence, and usually we realize it when it is too late. Good health is absolutely necessary for our journey, our dream and our life. Someone said if you have health you have everything and if you lose your health you lose everything. This statement can never get any truer. If you are sick, you can do little if anything; you can't work on your dream, much less on the job. You will fall behind on your bills. You will eventually pile up debts and this situation will strain your unhealthy physical state. There are people who, having accomplished their dreams and becoming successful in the great scheme of things, are incapable of enjoying the wealth, the power or the prestige that comes with their success because they are not in good physical conditions. I don't think they would consider themselves successful. There are also those who are quite incapable of providing for their family because the only place they are suited to stay is in hospitals or worse six feet under. How sad that is. These different situations are meant as a wake-up call to ponder on the matter of your health. I am not implying that you should worry about these eventualities, but rather it is a motivation to consider taking care of yourself as part of your overall goals. Don't we know that good health is so important for us and in fact for most people it is more important than material wealth? For those who are materially deprived, personal health is all they have.

When I call friends and family back home, they often complaint about how difficult things are, how they barely have enough to eat. I remember and know too well how that is, but in the end they assure me that they are healthy and that everybody is well. In certain societies where acquiring basic things is the everyday struggle, people grow accustomed to it and they strive to stay healthy. There was a time when I did not give much consideration when told they were well and healthy. I thought that they were merely saying it to place a positive spin on the conversation, but it dawned on me that being healthy is critically important for them. Imagine being sick and broke when life is difficult. This circumstance qualifies you as a dead man walking. When I was growing up as a child, it used to be a common practice in the village where we lived, that every first day of a new year, elders would come out of their huts early in the morning to sing the song of a new year. The song was to thank God for having allowed them to experience the new year in good health. Even though most villagers were living under cavemen-like conditions, most of them prayed for good health.

Cost of staying healthy is affordable for everybody

Staying healthy could be the cheapest investment you can make. Staying healthy requires awareness and a little bit of discipline. Doing small things every day can go a long way toward being healthy. For example, eating an apple a day may sound insignificant, but in the long run you will see the effect. It is important to get into the habit of making healthy nutritional choices. This doesn't mean one must only consume organic or natural food as such a practice may be too costly for some people. If you can afford it, that's great. But simply having a well-balanced diet will get you on the side of a healthy life style. For example, if you eat fruits, vegetables and grains, you will find some dietary balance. I read an article that put in simple mathematical terms how it is cost effective to include fruit in your daily diet. The article mentioned that the banana which is very rich in potassium costs about sixty nine cents a pound in most markets in the US. Therefore, one banana could cost about twenty three cents presuming that three bananas make a pound. This is just a simple illustration of how a well-balanced diet is not reserved for people with good fortune as many might think; anybody can afford to eat a healthy diet. Doing so requires a conscious decision and discipline.

Exercise is the preventive medicine

Another important way to develop a healthy lifestyle and determine success is to follow an exercise routine. Almost everyone recognizes exercise is important, however, one of my friends goes to great lengths to explain that exercising can never stop you from dying and he uses the example of an Italian soccer player who died from cardiac arrest during a game. With that reasoning, you could easily guess how healthy my friend is. I have yet to find someone else who thinks and believes that exercise is bad for you.

Yet numerous scientific researchers have found that it is in fact the key to staying healthy and living longer.

Physical activity does the following:

Improves your chance of living longer.
Helps protect against heart disease and high blood pressure.
Helps protect against the development of certain cancer cells.
Prevents type 2 diabetes and contains and manages type 1 diabetes.
Helps restore bone density and avoid osteoporosis.
Helps relieve the symptoms of depression and anxiety and improves mood.
Helps with weight loss.
Improves sleep.
Restores energy.

Many people are conscious of some benefits associated

with exercise, but few really engage in a consistent regime. The popular excuse people bring forward is time. They don't have time to exercise. People come up with all manner of excuses and justifications for why they can't exercise. It sounds bogus to me. Quite frankly, I don't see time as the problem, but I understand that people simply don't grasp the importance of exercise. Once you establish in your mind that this exercise will keep you away from doctors, you will find time. Exercise is preventive medicine. If the doctor bluntly tells you that you can die if you don't exercise, you will find a time. Maybe doctors need to start prescribing exercise to patients. I know some doctors do advise patients to exercise, but advice will never take on the power of a prescription. Simply, it doesn't seem as urgent as a prescription.

Exercise like nutritional regime doesn't have to be strict or harsh, but it must follow the principle of progressive overload. This simply means that it is important for safety reasons to start really small and gradually move toward bigger and harder exercises. Instead of trying to find one hour out of your free time, you can find fifteen minutes to start, possibly less. Science has shown that seven minutes is sufficient enough for the body to reap some benefits associated with exercise. During this portion of time, the brain secretes endorphins which are responsible for good mood.

Similarly, you don't have to buy a gym membership to start exercising. Some people wait for the right weather, the right time of the day. They are saving to buy the right tennis shoes, the right outfit or equipment. Some people even wait to start exercising until they find an exercise partner. You can start doing something, anything in the comfort of your bedroom, living room, or backyard; better yet, you can start walking around the block even with your work clothes still on. When you are ready to do more, start walking two blocks, then three blocks and so on. Soon enough you can start running and doing some calisthenics using your own body for strength. Few of such exercises include push-ups, pull ups, crunches, plank, squads, and lounges and so on. And each of these exercises has different variations for the sake of variety. It is important to avoid a routine that leads to the plateau known as "hitting a wall": It is a level at which the body no longer reaps the benefit resulting from certain exercises. The point is to get into the habit of doing something, to be self-disciplined enough and self-aware to consider exercise a part of your life.

A simple philosophy says everything affects everything. By becoming physically active and choosing the right foods, you will affect every area of your life.

When you are physically fit, you have greater confidence and a degree of authority. You will be self-assured and poised and more energetic. All these qualities are necessary for career success and even life success. Studies have shown that those with great physical fitness are more likely to be hired, to be promoted and to get salary increases.

I certainly started attracting attention with my fitness ability when I began to work out. I could tell that the number of people who befriended me increased as some of them were curious about my physical fitness. The interesting part was the fact that I became rather like an expert on the subject. People were asking me what my secret was, since I had eight packs. Some people were even curious as to what I ate. That curiosity prompted me to become a fitness trainer.

Yet my approach is simple. I never used a gym except for the period of six months when I received a free gym membership through an employer. My exercise regime is easy and simple. I exercise three times a week skipping a day or two for rest. During each session, I combine strength exercises and cardiovascular exercises, beginning with the former. There is a simple reason why I always start with strength exercise. The fast-twitch muscles used for the strength exercise draw energy from the body's simple sugars such as carbohydrates. By the time I start the cardiovascular exercise, the energy will be coming directly from the fat zone. Therefore, one can lose weight quicker.

The strength exercise consists of using my own body weight for each routine. This is called calisthenics exercise. It is important to do these exercises covering the upper body, the midsection and the lower body.

For the upper body you can do push-ups, pull-ups, dips and so on. For the midsection, exercises such as crunches, sit-ups and plank will provide results. For the lower body, squats, lunges and butt raises will work best. And of course there are different variations of these exercises and many other exercises that are effective for each part of the body.

After the strength exercise, which I accomplish in about 20 minutes, I spend at least 15 minutes to finish up my session with cardiovascular exercise that can be running, biking, swimming (seldom happens) or anything that has the potential to raise the heart beat and increase the heart rate.

In all, I could spend a bit over 30 minutes in exercise, and the result is there to see.

So don't think about doing it. Just do it.

Start doing something to become healthier today.

In my country there is this common belief: when you are bulky and the belly is hanging, that shows you are well fed and therefore you are living well. Conversely those who are skinny are malnourished and diseased. This is a very dangerous perspective and contrary to fact. That notion destroys peoples' incentive to become healthy.

When you start to become healthier, you will realize that other aspects of your life start to change too.

Chapter 5

What makes us Happy?

"Folks are usually about as happy as they make their mind to be"

— Abraham Lincoln

I first came to understand the deeper meaning of the concept of happiness when I read the part of the United States Declaration of Independence that says that we are endowed by our "Creator with certain unalienable Rights that among these are Life, Liberty and the pursuit of Happiness". I wondered why the notion of the "pursuit of happiness" was such a big deal. I thought "pursuit of happiness" was a phrase that you could throw around without much thought. Then, I started to give serious consideration what the words really mean. I would catch myself saying that I am happy. I soon realized that the state of happiness is always associated with something that has happened such as I am happy because I have a new car. It got me to think that happiness was conditioned to something. In other words, for me to be happy something positive had to happen. I started to notice that others manifested the feeling of happiness in the same way.

We often get caught up in this cause and effect gyration. We tell ourselves that we will be happy when we get that job, if we own a house, if we get that promotion. Curiously, when I had a promotion at my job, the one question my colleagues asked me was whether I was happy. I would say yes just to satisfy their curiosity, but in reality I was appreciative of the fact that my enthusiasm for life and willingness to do more than a job was recognized. The promotion didn't make me happy. I was promoted because I was a happy person.

Happiness seems like an end result of all our undertakings in life. Most of what we do is motivated by the desire to be happy. It is at the helm of our constant need for anything new; such as a new job, a new house, a new car, new clothes, and even a new partner. We get this feeling through recognition, validation and so on. It seems to be an ideal that we all strive to attain. While it is true that reaching our goals can provide us with a spark of joy or happiness, it won't be long before what was once new becomes old, when the initial element of attraction has lost its power. This concept is proven for situations where money is what we need to become happy. I am quite certain that you know of or have heard of people with money who are not happy. In fact we hear about it every day in the media when Hollywood celebrities who are loaded with money, check into rehabilitation centers.

On the same angle of the spectrum, studies have shown that lottery winners after about six months go back to the level of happiness where they were before winning. Sometimes they even become less happy. I want to dispel confusion here. I am not implying that "one doesn't buy happiness." What I'm saying is that if you condition your happiness solely on the acquisition of money, you could be disappointed. One perfect example would be the life story of Jordan Belfort, the writer and author of **The Wolf of Wall Street**. At one point in his life, he became one of the rainmakers on Wall Street possessing almost all the things money can buy, but according to his own testament he felt "empty." Life fulfillment is not just about money. I use money only as an example because it is the one thing many in the world pursue, since with money one can afford things that provide a fringe of happiness. But when we hit that cul-de-sac, we find ourselves again looking for places or things to provide happiness, and the cycle begins once more. This is the true reality which we live day in and day out.

We relapse because the object of our happiness has lost its value. We fall victims to the many paradigms in our society where attainment of happiness is concerned. I have observed that celebrations tend to satisfy that desire to be happy. Let's take Valentine's Day, for example, which is supposed to be the celebration of the loved ones. Although nothing is wrong with celebrating, the way that we have fashioned those moments, it seems as if we need to wait for times like that to be happy with the love ones. Frankly, the show of great love doesn't have to wait for a specific moment to be celebrated. The love of loved ones can be done every day. It is the same with Christmas. The commercialization of this day has become so intense that many celebrate Christmas without understanding the true meaning behind it. The way our society has made it, it seems as though it is a day when everyone should be happy, with the gifts and presents flying left and right, families and friends enjoying time together with all the commotion surrounding the event. Again, there is nothing wrong with that. The problem is that many people project their moment of happiness to circumstances and attribute happiness to happenstance. Happiness seems to be something outside of themselves, an ideal to pursue.

It is the unfortunate truth that many don't even attain what they desire and consequently they fall into a pit of stress and despair.

Happiness is a choice, a decision.

The dictionary defines happiness as mental or emotional state of well-being characterized by positive or pleasant emotions ranging from contentment to intense joy. Our mental state should not be conditioned by exterior factors such as our conditions or conditioning and our environment. There is an element of choice here and that element is most important because it is the one that guarantees a long and lasting positive emotion. Other exterior elements that are factors of pleasant emotions are quite ephemeral. I mentioned earlier the examples of basing happiness on possessing something or arriving somewhere, how these elements have the tendency to lose their attractiveness. As immigrants, we were initially driven by the desire for a better life; that prompted us to leave our respective countries. When we were still back home, we had this idea that America was beyond utopia. We thought of it as a terrestrial paradise where everything was made of gold; figuratively, it seemed the manna that fell in Egypt about two thousand years ago was again falling. It seemed all was wonderful in the best of all possible worlds; therefore, it was a place where happiness was everlasting. We thought everyone was rich and successful there. However, a few months after we arrived, we started facing a paradigm shift that would eventually lead to disappointment. The few first moments are usually filled with intense joy upon arriving at the country of dreams, but it is soon replaced by frustration. Even though the conditions in this country are far better than conditions in the country of origin, many immigrants fail to capitalize on the privilege; only a few realize that there is still gold and that it is hidden in plain sight.

Disappointments and frustrations generally stem from unrealistic expectations. This is true wherever you live. Friends and clients often seek my advice about the problems that threaten to destroy relationships and marriages. In most cases, I simply point out the disappointment resulting from expectations. So unrealistic expectations are at the bottom of many misunderstandings; one expects the other to conform to certain thinking and beliefs, sometimes without any discussion. I am not an expert in marriage counseling, but I see unrealistic expectations as a serious problem.

Our happiness should not depend upon circumstances. What I mean is we should not be happy *because* this thing or that thing happens. We should think of happiness as a decision we make for ourselves. Yes, happiness is a deliberate choice. We can choose to be happy today. It is a simple, yet powerful approach that requires proper reasoning.

A friend who was going through tough times argued that I was teaching a nonsensical approach. She reasonably asked how one could become happy when nothing had seemed to work for years. She had struggled as far back as she could remember. She didn't think life was fair. I couldn't disagree with her; life is often unfair, but she ended the argument by mentioning that everything was in the hands of God —thanks God for that. This was how the argument moved to the subject of God whom she believed was in charge of all things. But the question she could not answer was: why worry if God is in charge? If we believe that God is at the center of our lives, then hardship and struggle should be seen as His way of acting in our lives. Therefore, we should be happy that we have the Almighty at our side fighting to win the battle for us.

Often times, we overlook the simple thing that we can use to pull out of despair. More to the point, we can choose to be happy now. It really is as simple as it sounds. Usually our expectation is that a complex problem requires a complex solution. We tend to travel miles to find the solution to a specific situation when, most of the time, the solution is at our fingertips.

Naturally, being happy is difficult if one loses a job, if we are going through a divorce or even when things are simply not going the way we want. Of course when looking at our lives that way, being happy seems like backward logic. Therefore, we can't imagine the solution is so simple.

It is true we can't control conditions, circumstances and events that happen to us. You cannot control whether your service is no longer needed after many decades of employment. You cannot control whether your spouse falls in love with somebody else. You have to understand that according to Murphy's Law, anything that can go wrong will go wrong at the worst possible time.

But we possess the ultimate freedom to respond to what happens to us. We can smile or we can frown; the choice is ours. Nobody can deprive us of that ability. You are in full control. You shouldn't give that control away. You should try to look at the opportunity behind what happens. Sometimes you only need to realize that by losing your job, the universe might be giving you the chance to work on that dream of yours. Perhaps you have been putting it off for many years. I have a friend who, after losing his job as a sales associate, went on to build his international trade business. He prospered doing something he previously only talked about.

Whatever is happening to us may be an opportunity in disguise. If we look at it from different angles instead of wallowing in despair, we might welcome the possibilities.

Things That Can Make Us Happy

Choosing to be happy can also take the form of active engagement. Science has proven that certain activities can increase our level of happiness. Some of those activities include:

Exercise

Just a few minutes of exercise are enough to cause the brain to start releasing endorphins, which are the body's natural morphine. Endorphins are responsible for good mood. Many athletes have experienced a moment of euphoria called the *runner's high* during their athletic activities. Many have reported having this feeling when they have pushed themselves to the point of exhaustion. But the good news is; you don't have to engage in intense or a full-hour-long workout to achieve that goal. A mere seven minutes of exercise, science says, is enough for us to feel good about ourselves.

Reaching our goals through exercise will increase our level of happiness. If we set out to lose weight, our new body will provide us with self-confidence and self-assurance.

Smile

Smiling is another way of improving your happiness. Smiling and happiness can be interchangeable in a sense because people know that you are happy because you are smiling, and they know you are smiling because you are happy. But such may not always be the case. A fake smile doesn't always mean that the author is happy. There is a nuance. A study reveals a mechanical effect occurs in the brain when you fake a smile. In fact, in a study which was conducted at a university campus, students held a pencil between their teeth without the lips touching the pencil. With this position, the muscles around the mouth curl in the position of a smile, and immediately the brain goes to work to deliver the positive effect. The brain does not distinguish between what is fake and what is real. Any movement that affects the facial muscles, precisely the ones around the mouth and eyes, will trigger the brain's reaction. The brain thinks that you are smiling. So by faking a smile, we are giving the brain an opportunity to react positively. You can therefore fake it in order to make it. Try to see if this approach has merit by faking a smile during a stressful situation. I am quite certain that your mood will be altered.

Smiling has the reverse positive effect on the author. The mechanism of mirror neurons is a reaction in our brain that causes us to mimic the emotions of others. When we smile, whether genuine or not, the person will return the smile which in turn reinforces our state of contentment. Smiling is like energy that bounces back and returns to the source.

In life, one of the most rewarding things that we do is to help someone who is a worse off than us. This principle applies with the gift of smiling. When you know that your smile has brightened someone else's day, you feel happier and you feel rewarded.

I have to be frank about what the smile has done for me. I am a big guy of six feet four. I have an imposing physical frame. Sometimes I dress casually —borderline street dress— and I observe that some people appear uncomfortable until I flash my greatest smile; then people loosen up and become curious and eager to engage in conversation. A smile for me is the extinguisher that puts out fire; it is the small fire that can warm the heart.

I smile a lot and have experienced the effect of a smile on myself. Smiling is therapeutic for me. Anytime I feel a bit confused, overwhelmed or stressed, I smile for no particular reason and immediately my mood changes to become positive. I use it when I have migraine headaches, and it works like magic. I don't remember the last time I took a pill for a headache. It was probably decades ago. As of the writing of this book, I rarely have bad days. Now, I even use a smile to help other people by touching their heart. I often get about 98% genuine return smiles. When you genuinely smile at people, you pull them into your lightness. I have been given the name *"Sunshine"* by different people in reference to how often I smile. Smiling is part of my personality.

Practicing a smile is easy and simple. Yet, once smiling becomes a habit, it can transform your life completely. Most of humanity assumes that a happy person is a loving person.

Gratitude

Another way to increase our happiness is by showing gratitude. The expression "Thank you" is another way to express gratitude. But saying, Thank you" has lost its intrinsic significance in our society today. We can say it ten times in the course of a day, without meaning it. Saying, "Thank you" can be like saying the courteous word, "Please." Almost everybody in the world is taught to say, "Please" when appropriate. But saying the word doesn't necessarily mean that the person is courteous, because some people say, "Please" or "Thank you" with clenched teeth. I am not saying that there is no genuine expression of, "Thank you" in our world today, but often the expression is merely a filler. Sometimes the expression is used at the close of a conversation. I have heard people robotically say, "Thank you," and I am guilty of that on many occasions.

Gratitude may be felt whether or not it is uttered. Gratitude is a deep recognition of something in our life that was not required. When we are aware of that, it gives us a sense of appreciation. Through feeling gratitude, our mood is boosted. While the attitude of gratitude is not commonplace, it is simple in its application. We easily grow accustomed to things in our lives and develop a sense of entitlement which is not necessarily a bad thing, but it can prevent us from knowing that things could be different. We all are guilty of this lack of gratitude at one point or another. But gratitude is a learnable habit. We need to increase our level of awareness. You can begin to practice the attitude of gratitude early every morning for a new day that is rising and at the end of the day no matter what transpired. You can also begin to appreciate your spouse for something good you notice about him or her. You can thank your children for making you a better person with their constant rebellious attitude. You can thank your enemy for challenging you to become better, and the list can go on and on. As far as life is concerned the situation could have been worse. It is important to recognize that those who are religiously inclined have a good understanding of this notion of gratitude. They thank God for the gift of life:

They thank God that they asked for strength and He gave them difficulties to make them strong.
They thank God that they asked for wisdom and He gave them problems to solve.
They give thanks to God that they asked for favor and He gave them opportunities.

But you don't have to be a believer in God to recognize and appreciate all the wonders of life and to recognize that a sort of synergy is constantly at work and making your life possible.

These few steps are only the tip of an iceberg when it comes to improving our happiness. A wide range of small things can make us happy. We can find for ourselves things that work.

When I was going through what seemed to be helpless moments in my life, one thing kept me going. It was hope.

I have always believed that tomorrow will be better than today even when I had no idea how it was going to be different. What makes me happy today is the belief that no situation is permanent.

Happiness also comes from hoping that what we are doing today will lead to the desired outcome. Happiness is simply about enjoying the process. Sometimes the journey is more enjoyable than arriving at the destination. I mentioned earlier the example of preparation for a holiday like Christmas. I have observed over the years that people are enthusiastic when preparing for Christmas with decorations everywhere; music is playing in most houses and on most radio stations and television channels. Moments of collective happiness add to the individual's happiness.

A simple exercise can help us during stressful moments. It is called *emotional recall*.

When things go wrong and we find ourselves drifting, grasping for a good feeling, we can do the following:

Close your eyes (preferably) and think of a past positive experience, sit quietly and remember the circumstances, where you were, who else was there, what time it was, the sound, the smell and concentrate on what happened and how you felt, feel it as though it were happening again. You will realize that you are reliving the moment and the same feeling you felt will rush back and fill your soul, mind and body.

When we feel happy by choice or by taking action our energy is added to the energy frequency of the universe and the law of attraction takes effect.

The law of attraction simply says that like attracts like, meaning in this case, that when we are happy, the universe will see that we are provided with more things and circumstances that will continue to keep us in that state of mind. We must remember that everything is energy, and that through the law of attraction, we attract to us what we predominantly think about or feel.

Chapter 6

The Impact of Surroundings

"You are the average of five people you spend the most time with."

— Jim Rohn

We are social animals and destined to live in society unless we decide to do otherwise. Association with other people is important to our success and happiness. It is the interrelation with others that is the hallmark of human life. Studies have recorded that loneliness or life in isolation can kill faster than smoking. Therefore, those who develop a strong social web such as family and friends are likely to live longer than those who don't. So we are called to be and live together not only by our nature, but also for our own life's sake. We are interconnected to one another by shared humanity.

Family

As Africans, we consider family to be anyone who has a direct or indirect tie to us through blood or marriage. The family members usually consist of parents, siblings, aunts and uncles, cousins, nieces and nephews and so on. These are the people we interact with on a regular basis, and they have direct impact on our lives. They play a significant role in our growth and development. Sometimes the impact that our family has on us is not positive. A good relationship with family members is a blessing for our lives, but the lack of a good relationship can constitute a curse. For instance, a father can easily curse a son or daughter who doesn't respect family traditions and wishes. I grew up in a very traditional family where a good relationship with all family members even with those who had passed away was vitally important. Those who had passed away were the most influential because they possess the supernatural powers that those living don't possess. They can act in ways that are unknown to the living.

Family is the primary cell of the society, and it is an element of our social identity. In society at large, we are who we are in relation to our family. We pick up traits from our family that will stay with us throughout our lives. Some of those traits could be genetic. For instance, we pick up physical characteristics and mental qualities from our parents and grandparents. The physical characteristics can be height, size and so on. If your genes predispose you to be tall, you could aspire to be a basketball player where height is a definite plus.

The same characteristic applies on the emotional level. If your parents were abusive for instance, there is a tendency that you could become abusive unless you exercise your freedom to choose otherwise.

Another element given by our family is a name or a

nickname. This element is very instrumental and can influence our lives. That is why many people give a great deal of thought when choosing a name for their offspring. The beauty of the name appeals to some families, but the meaning is the most important factor in choosing the name. Many families select the names of great celebrities, great presidents, influential people of the present and past. They intend for their offspring to pick up some qualities of the person for whom they have been named. After Barack Obama became president of the United States of America, many new-born babies around the world were given the name Obama. When we are grownups with the name of an influential individual, there is sometimes pressure to live up to our name or to carry the name well by doing something important in our lives.

I certainly have felt that way when people remind me that I have one of the greatest names they have ever heard. My full name is Elvis Prince Tognia, but there is no direct connection to Elvis Presley, the king of Rock & Roll or even Prince, the other famous singer. (Some people joke that Elvis' song was playing when I was conceived). Elvis Presley was not popular where I was born as television didn't yet exist in my country, and radio was at an early stage of development. My mom told me that there was another Elvis in my country at that time who was also a singer, and she liked the name. That is the origin of my name.

But I feel a certain urge to carry this name well by doing something significant and meaningful in my life. This name along with the nickname my grandmother gave me has had a good impact on my life. My nickname is

Noumen Guessagi. In my native language it means, "You will never have more than you can handle." This nickname has carried me through challenges since the moment I was born. When one door shuts in my life, there always seems to be another door opening.

The name you bear can be a motivation if you have awareness, but it can become a hindrance. Those who wear names such as Osama Ben Laden, or Hitler can be hindered. After September 11 2014, there was resentment toward anyone wearing a name that resembled the masterminds behind the attack.

Almost every name has significance. Many dictionaries define names, especially if the name is from Western civilization. It is worthwhile to refer to a dictionary of names. Once you become aware of the significance of your name, there will be a subconscious effort to reconcile your life with your name, especially if there is a positive connotation.

We can acquire from our family their beliefs, traditions and practices. Although things are now starting to change, in the past and in certain families even today, children often follow in their parent's footsteps. If you are born into certain religious families, the family religion will be yours by default. Children often continue the parents' business; they usually attend the same school and work the same type of job. Often they become what the parents expect them to be.

But we need to be aware of the ability to develop our endowments. We can use our independent will and imagination to shift from what we are accustomed to, and we can choose a different path for ourselves. This is really important because while our family may want the best for us, what they want may not be what we want for ourselves.

But no matter the path we choose for ourselves, I believe we should remain family centered because that is the source of great motivation in life.

For me, everything revolves around family. It is why I do what I do. In my family, no one has achieved success. No one is able to take the lead financially. When problems arise, I must assume a leadership role. After all, I am the only one who has been giving the opportunity to travel abroad. It is my responsibility to take care of the family. I remember the day I was traveling to the Unites States of America, almost the entire family, more than 30 people, came to the airport to say goodbye. I am their hope, their bridge, their transitional person. They count on me to reverse the family's century old state of poverty. For this reason, I draw motivation from them to do what I can to fulfill that hope.

There are those who do well in life because they want to offer to their children the opportunity to obtain a good education in the best public and private schools. Others pursue and achieve big goals because they want to take care of their parents by buying them a house or offering them the opportunity to go on vacation to their favorite places. I've heard of a man who was the only sibling his parents could afford to send to school. He did so well in life that he created a scholarship program to give opportunity to others like his siblings who had less of a chance to continue their education.

Sometimes, we want to do well to match or surpass the achievements of those who have come before us and set a precedent. It is common in our society to hear of children trying to equal their parents or surpass them.

Every day brings with it the opportunity to make things better for my children and to provide an education and other opportunities to reverse generations of poverty. My family causes me to take action. If there is a day when I am slacking off, which happens from time to time, I remember that my mom might be hungry and the fear makes me get pumped up and charged up. After such fears and thoughts about my family, I make bold moves.

Any person can use family to be motivated and accomplish outstanding results.

Some people may not rely on family as their source of motivation, but family is still how they evaluate success. Just imagine working hard your entire life to acquire material success. What if you accumulate substantial wealth, possess big mansions and have all the toys, but there isn't anybody to share it with because you have alienated them. How unbalanced such a life would be. I doubt such a life would qualify as successful.

Surround Yourself with Like-Minded People

Friends and colleagues play an important role in our lives depending upon how close they are to us. When we surround ourselves with a group of people who are great fans and support us in our undertakings, it can propel us to attain heights of achievement. They keep us accountable for our promises and actions. In order to be accountable for your actions, it is sometimes necessary to tell friends, family and the public about your goals. It will oblige you to keep your word or suffer the consequences of shame, ridicule and loss of trust.

Friendship should be nurtured and friends should benefit each other. There is no lasting quality for a friendship that is calculated or premeditated. In these kinds of friendship, one person uses the other to arrive at an end. Actions are executed at another's expense. Unfortunately, our society has grown to be governed by a paradigm where the pursuit of egoistic self-interest and fierce competition dictate that we must use all means necessary to arrive on top. This maxim is widespread simply because some people arrive at the top using those means, but those successes usually become a quagmire. Good friendship based on mutual respect and mutual benefit always thrives and is at the foundation of many successes. The same principle applies to associates or work partners.

But friendship can also be detrimental to one's success. Friends like family can be dream killers. Some friends simply do not appreciate what you see in your dreams. They may think your dream is crazy. They are simply expressing opinions. Know that everyone has opinions to express to anyone who is willing to listen. Although well intentioned sometimes, the opinions of others can have the effect of stifling your objectives and ambitions. Some people will only believe your idea is possible if they know that someone else has achieved it. And this is true to all human beings. This general belief system is well illustrated by the fact that, before 1954, it was humanly impossible to break the four-minute mile run. It was tried time and again with failure. Then, Roger Banister broke the record. From that time to this day more than twenty thousand people have broken the record including high school students. The question is what changed? Practically nothing has changed. But every time someone stepped behind the starting line, they believed that it had been done before and that they too could do it. So people operate by what they see, hear and believe is possible. Some friends will not believe in your dream because they don't understand it. Perhaps your dream is not as familiar as a dream of being a teacher, a doctor or lawyer.

When I expressed my intention of becoming a public speaker, many friends ridiculed me saying that I am a "reveur" meaning a "dreamer" in the pejorative sense of the term. Most of them didn't know what motivational speaking meant. They wondered if it was a job, and they wondered what one does as a public speaker. I tried to explain what public speaking entails. I wanted to make them see what I saw, to make them feel what I felt. I wanted so badly to win their approval. I wanted someone to tell me that I was on the right path and to cheer me up. But I was completely wrong. They would go through a litany of reasons why I didn't have what it took to become a public speaker. They argued that I didn't have a "public title" as if there were a requirement that a public figure be successful or rich. Some would say that we are Africans and Africans don't come to the US to dream. I would also hear that I am a French speaker. I would work ten times harder in the language department just to be at the level of the average English-born competitor. One of my friends went out of his way to tell me that it is almost impossible to become a big fish in the pond without meshing with sectarian milieus. He used the example of specific celebrities; singers and actors saying they sold their souls to the devil. He also added government officials and executives to the list. According to him anyone who has ever reached the ladder of success has done something beyond what is normal and that unless I become part of an exceptional circle, I can't amount to anything big.

Imagine that you have this particular dream and it isn't yet strong .The safest route after hearing these arguments would be for you to quickly forget your dream and find another one that is more acceptable to your friends. You must recognize that if you are the smartest person in your group, it is time for you to get a new group. If your friends are not smart enough to see your dream or support you in it, it is wise to be more selective when choosing friends.

As you take a new direction in life to become better and dream big, you have to be careful of those you associate with because, "Birds of a feather flock together."

If you associate with negative people, soon enough your ambitions, goals and dreams will be choked off. This truth can be likened to the parable of the sower in the Bible. When the sower sowed the seeds, some grain felt between the thorns. When the seeds sprouted, the thorns choked them and they died. Your dream is just like that grain; when it starts to grow, negatives friends will kill it with their negativity. That is why you must protect your dreams against certain types of people. One of the safest ways is to make new friends or to associate with like-minded people. Associate with those who have similar dreams, who think the way you do. Associate with those who offer constructive criticism. Avoid those who express only negative opinions to anyone with creative goals.

It is not easy to dispose of some friends. It is more difficult to part with family. Maybe you grew up with a certain friend; maybe the friend helped you at a point in the past; maybe the friend is close to your family and you find it almost impossible to part with them. I believe if your dream is strong enough and if someone is a hindrance, you are obligated to let that friend go and suffer the consequences. Otherwise, you cannot let them influence your dreams.

If you cannot completely erase them from your circle, you can take certain approaches that will provide distance so they don't have so much influence on you and your dreams: If, for instance, you are used to talking to them many times during a day or week, how about progressively reducing the frequency of your talks or visits to once a day or once a week. It is not selfish to get rid of your friends in order to pursue what is meaningful to you. This attitude should not to be confused with selfishness. Self-interest says you are unique, that you have greatness within you, that your contribution to this world will be important, and that you have a mission to accomplish before you die. You are not pursuing it to the detriment of others. You would be doing a disservice to many people including your friends if you let their influence stop you from accomplishing your mission.

Some friends will be negative out of jealousy and envy because you are doing something that they cannot figure out for themselves. Don't worry about them. You will grow away from them as a result of pursuing your goals and they will retire from your life because you no longer have anything in common.

During the process of my transformation, I didn't have many friends, and I was glad I didn't because they would have been distractions. To have to constantly talk to them on the phone or return their phone calls or get together to watch games would have been time consuming. An exception would exist if there was an opportunity to grow. The one thing I would do was to get together with friends to play soccer every Saturday. Undoubtedly, the benefit of growing was tremendous. I would use that opportunity to exercise because I did not have a chance to exercise during the week. All things considered, there is not really much I can do after working a full time job and taking care of four kids. I had to be very selective about extra activities.

There is one important question that needs to be addressed in terms of how to separate from negative people. Is the negative person, the naysayer, a spouse or a partner, a parent or a child?

Of course, it is almost impossible to stay away from home and avoid the negativity of family. To give up on dreams because of a desire to please others will be fatal to your success. You must find ways that work in your situation and keep pursuing your dreams. Suppose you have a spouse or partner who is not supportive but gives you free range to pursue your activities. You will have the opportunity to prove to them that you can achieve your dream. That becomes your motivation.

You may have a situation where your spouse or your partner not only doesn't support you but he or she nags you, insults you, disrespects you or even wishes you failure by not giving you the opportunity to prove that your dream can work. This case requires that one treads cautiously. It is tempting to abandon your dreams and try to satisfy your partner to save your relationship. But if your dream is strong enough you must do lots of growing here. You must cultivate skills such as patience, tolerance, forgiveness and focus. I have lived such moments. I know how it is to leave in the morning already physically and mentally exhausted because of negativity. You have to develop a mental wall to protect your sanity and your ambitions; you have to grow a thick skin. Without the skills previously mentioned, it will be impossible to escape that situation unscathed.

You also need to find ways to balance the negative atmosphere at home by being among those who inspire you to maintain a positive attitude and to be productive. You can do this by attending different interest groups that may inspire your growth and development. You can even create a group where you have control. This could be called your mastermind group.

Establishing such a group can accelerate your growth. The idea is to have a group of people who come together on a regular basis —weekly, monthly or yearly— to share ideas and thoughts, and to exchange information and resources. This process can help offset down moments and further your progress.

Our Environment Can Facilitate Our Success in Life

What surrounds you can motivate you to do outstanding things and to live your best life or what surrounds you can kill initiative. This is to say, where you live or work can influence your chance to have a fulfilling life.

Unfortunately, it is impossible to choose the country where you are born and it's not easy to leave your home and live in another country because of laws and regulations that each country has to protect its borders and its citizens within its territorial borders. But if it is possible to go elsewhere to develop one's potential, one shouldn't hesitate. Every day there is migration from the undeveloped countries to the most industrialized ones. Frankly, I sometimes wonder what I might have become had I stayed in my country of origin. I would have amounted to nothing since I came from a very poverty-stricken family with no connections, no power and no money. I would have been doomed to be a social pariah. There is little opportunity for great accomplishment and success in a poor country.

Even within a country there are variations of influence on an individual's success depending on the city where they live. If, for example, you aspire to be an actor or model or an entertainer in the US, certain cities like Los Angeles, New York or Chicago offer more opportunities. You have less chance of success when living in a small town in Alaska. In the same vein, if you want to be a lobbyist, Washington, D.C. would be the ideal place for you. Still, even inside the city there are neighborhoods that are more favorable to your success, depending on what you want to pursue. Statistics show that children living in inner cities have less chance of success than those living in neighborhoods like Beverly Hills, Bel Air and Malibu, all cities within the County of Los Angeles. So if you can afford to live in such a place, it is a great investment because, the people you associate with will play an important role in helping you become the best you can be. The logic holds true also regarding the school you attend. When given a chance, most people will attend an Ivy League school. Besides its prestigious title, such institutions are well-respected around the world and therefore guarantee alumni a degree of success.

Being where there is opportunity can motivate you to grow and become successful.

When I came to the USA, I landed in the Washington, D.C. area where I spent about six years. I followed what others did, whether it was going to school or creating the idea of my future which was far from certain. There is a large African Diaspora living in D.C. Metropolitan, which means that the way of life in each community is not far from the way Africans lived in their home countries. We attended regular meetings to discuss important matters or to socialize. We often spoke our language of origin, ate foods from home and behaved as if we were still in Africa. This sort of life in community is great for those who are transitioning, but this life can result in lack of full integration. That was what I started to feel. I wanted to reinvent myself, to have freedom of mind. I wanted more. I felt I had to distinguish myself a little bit from my community where I had less opportunity to practice English as I was surrounded by those who spoke French and my dialect Medumba. I yearned for something different and big. So I decided that I had to go to another state or city. One day I packed my car and drove to Los Angeles even though I didn't know a soul there. I was driven by the spirit of adventure to discover new opportunities. Through trials and tribulations, I finally discovered the one thing that I wanted to do with the rest of my life. I wanted to be in the city and among people who would enhance my growth.

Our choice of where we live and whom we associate will determine success.

Any time that we procrastinate, we are denying those who might benefit from our greatness.

Chapter 7

The Importance of Faith

"All I have seen teaches me to trust the Creator for all I have not seen."
— *Ralph Waldo Emerson*

When you are ready for a new journey, you must take into account all that is necessary for its accomplishment. You must believe in and trust the path that you have to travel; trust yourself regarding your ability to take on the journey; trust those who help you along the way and most importantly, hope that all of these elements will take you to your destination. I am referring to faith. We can call upon our faith at every moment of our lives. Many people make a mistake and solely associate the notion of faith with religiosity. They think that when you mention faith, you automatically allude to God. While faith can refer to belief in God, it can also reference anything or any person you trust including yourself. Faith is a characteristic of human beings. Faith is one of our strongest and positive emotions. With faith there is peace, joy and hope. Without it life is hopeless.

The Effect of Hope

As an adult, I realize that faith has always been at the center of my life. I had faith even when I didn't have a straightforward relationship with God, and it was strengthened when I was able to discover Him. I had a very rough childhood. The hardship I endured resulted from intense poverty. We had almost nothing. We were not the poorest in the village but we were among the poorest, and I am not talking poverty by Western standards. It is one thing to be poor in a society where there are opportunities, but it is another thing when you are poor and live in a society with no opportunities. We had to borrow or beg for things like food, school supplies and clothes. Hope got me through each day; I simply hoped that tomorrow would be better even if I didn't know how it was going to change. I hoped for the unseen. Somehow I always believed that one day, things would be different. Maybe that is what anybody would feel when they find themselves at rock bottom. When you are completely down, your thoughts can only travel one way, and that is toward a better outcome. I believe that no situation is permanent, that every circumstance will pass. So when we find ourselves in impossible situations, we should reinforce our belief that things will get better. Sometimes we don't need to understand the logic behind hope. Hope manifests itself when we plant the seeds under the ground and trust that they will grow and bear fruit. We let the Power of Nature work its magic and it always does. We don't have control of the entire process, but we trust we will get what we desire. We must trust that what we want in life will be realized if we apply ourselves. When you begin a journey, you must trust that you will arrive at your chosen destination.

Faith is the fuel of persistence. You have to trust that no matter how hard it is, you are going to make it. Faith will take you through obstacles, bring you back from setbacks and cultivate resilience.

A great illustration of the power of faith is the ingenuity of Thomas A. Edison. He failed ten thousand times before getting the light bulb right. How many times would you fail before you stop? History can provide us with innumerable individuals who have employed the principle of faith to accomplish remarkable things.

Faith is a state of mind characterized by the acceptance of a thing as true.

Faith is manifested when we face challenges or obstacles or temporary failure. During those times logic can seem useless and our human reasoning can complicate the situation. Faith is the fuel of any undertaking. Without faith, we are unlikely to arrive at our desired destination. I believe faith is part of our being because all of us have called upon faith at some point. We use faith all the time, and sometimes we use it unknowingly.

Faith makes the difference between those who are successful at their undertakings and those who aren't. When doubt creeps in, it shatters everything. A passage in the Bible illustrating the power of faith describes Jesus walking on the surface of the water to join his disciples in the boat. When Peter saw him, he called out to Jesus and wanted to go to him. Jesus instructed him to join him and immediately Peter started walking on the surface of the water too. But when the wind started to blow violently, he became afraid and began to sink (Matthew 14: 22-33). So as soon as you let self-doubt overtake you, you will fall. You must have a firm conviction regarding where you are going and trust that you will get there. You have to trust yourself, trust your destination and trust the path that you believe will lead you to that destination.

Faith has always been my shield and my weapon of choice. I have to trust that any idea that I consider is the result of my own conclusion. But trusting myself has never been easy because of how I grew up. When you grow up in constant lack and deprivation, it is easy to trust the advice of someone who is better off. Your own opinion doesn't seem to matter; otherwise, you would not be where you are. You lose your autonomy. It is regrettable that many people give up on their dreams and believe the opinions of others. Such was my experience at one point in my life. I would believe anything a person with great wealth told me. Who was I to argue when I didn't even have food to eat? When the idea of becoming a professional speaker came to me, I filed it away in the back of my mind as quickly as it appeared. I seriously doubted myself. More to the point, friends and family thought I was a joke and a loser. I had yet to find an African professional speaker in the United States, especially one whose native language was not English. My internal dialogue almost derailed me. Then, I had to reason that if an idea came to me naturally, there must be some true foundation to it. It must have come from God, the source. I thought I must have faith in any noble idea that is meaningful and that can help me be of service to mankind. That was how I revised my dream and went to work for it.

Conscious Application of Faith

The most important point about faith is to be able to grow. As I mentioned, faith is part of our being, and we must be aware of it and consciously apply it in our lives. For example, if you believe in God, which I am not imposing on anyone, there are opportunities to increase your faith by involving yourself in your church's activities. You could also increase your church attendance. It is likely that you will become more devoted and therefore your faith will increase, too. Unless you are merely putting on a show, you will gain knowledge of God and develop increased faith that He will help you through any difficulty. Research shows that people who are active in their church tend to possess more faith than those people who only attend services.

Maybe you only pray in the comfort of your home; maybe you only pray when you think about it; maybe you always find the right time or the right place to pray. I have learned that there is no "best" time to pray. Many people would say that they pray when they wake up and before they go to bed at night, which is great. In fact it sounds like an ideal way given the fact that a morning prayer helps you go through the day, and the night prayer helps you through the night. As believers, if we think that God is present in our lives at all times, we should be able to talk to Him any moment during the day.

I have heard people say that being a believer doesn't help to be saved. They think that people hide behind institutions like churches to do wrong. People often point to an example of a good Christian who is the poster child of the devil, who corrupts, cheats, lies or even kills. An international scandal has been revealed concerning pastors and priests who perpetrate abuses on children.

We should understand that when the worst in human kind is exuded on the surface, it doesn't have anything to do with what one believes and where they belong.

There is another area where we must exercise autonomy. Our life should not depend on other people. The opinions and actions of others should not determine our behavior. We must know who we are and what we want. And nothing should change that.

Pascal advised belief in God because if he doesn't exist, you will not have lost anything, but if you believe in God and God does exist, you will have gained his favor. This philosophy can provide motivation.

How we pray is very important. I used to just utter words of prayer. It became like an automatic song. I used to feel empty after praying, but now I afterward feel energized.

Everybody believes in something. There is more to this life than the known physical aspect. As human, we often crave for more in our lives; we want to be fulfilled and enlightened. Unfortunately, these desires cannot be accomplished with the tangible. In our society, it is commonplace to see people who have accumulated enough riches for many generations and yet there is a void in their lives.

Faith and Belief in Africa

Every individual, group or society possesses a unique

way to practice their faith. I grew up as a Christian. I grew up believing in God through Jesus Christ. I attended Catholic school. But there was a moment growing up when faith didn't apply.

Africans used to believe in different gods in accordance with traditions established long before colonialism brought Christianity. Those practices and beliefs continued and remained even when colonialism was over. The majority of Africans who believed in God through Jesus Christ worshipped other gods at the same time. What was amazing was that even within an individual country, each tribe had their own gods. The ritual worship ceremony often varies from one tribe to another. I grew up with those practices. The worship of God through Christ didn't cancel the belief in other gods. A sign demonstrating the worship of other gods can be seen next to each house among certain tribes or families. There are small huts with walls five feet high and about six square feet of floor space. Inside those small huts reside the skulls of the ancestors that have been removed from the grave site and brought home. From time to time following a very special ritual, the ancestors are given food prepared in a special way. In the village where I grew up most inhabitants had an "ancestry" house in their compound. And everyone had their unique way of relating to their dead. Other families or tribes worship trees. Some worship rocks and so on. I cannot say with certainty that these practices have any effect. Who am I to judge people's beliefs? I will say those people seem to have peace, and often problems like illness, a curse or bad fate seem to disappear.

My dad when he was still alive, suffered horrifically

from bad fate. He had been ill for a very long time. He visited hospitals in the city where he, my mom and my siblings lived. I was living in a village with my grandmother. Doctors couldn't diagnose his illness. They just couldn't see anything wrong with him, yet he had lost a good deal of weight and was dying. He was barely walking because his feet were swollen and no medicine could help. He had a cough that never went away. He visited hospitals in other cities with no positive outcome. He tried traditional and modern medicine, but the disease persisted. As a last resort, he was advised by someone considered a charlatan to visit his ancestors. He traveled to the village where his ancestors had resided. As if by a wave of a magic wand, all symptoms started to slowly disappear. All he did was to prepare food for the ancestors and have a conversation with them. No other medicine was taken.

This sort of experience happens all the time to people in Africa. People follow these practices to undo any difficult challenge in life, whether it concerns finances, relationships, health or career.

The Miracle of Faith

Wonders happen when we believe. One day in October 2008, I came out of the library in Santa Monica on Ocean Park Avenue. I was leaving the sidewalk to cross 22nd Street to the bike lane on the other side of the road when a Lexus sedan made a right turn onto Ocean Park Avenue and struck me. Because the lady driving the car was looking over her shoulder at the oncoming cars, she didn't stop at the stop sign. I fell off the bicycle in front of the car.

Sensing that she might have hit something, she stopped. She came out of the car to check. At that point she saw me pinned under the car. It so happened that the car's front right tire ran over my right foot and came to rest on my right thigh above the knee. I was screaming hysterically. When she saw that I was under the car and that the tire was resting on my thigh, she panicked. She jumped left and right trying to signal for help. People who gathered barked at her to get in the car and back it off of me. By the time she did that, the ambulance and firefighters were on the scene. I got up. I felt fine and my foot seemed ok. I started to walk although the paramedics insisted that I should not move. Ironically, I was very concerned about my bike which was badly bent up on the side of the road. The ambulance attendants strapped me on a stretcher and took me to the Emergency Room at Saint John's Hospital in Santa Monica. I was released two hours later with only a few bruises on the side of my knee. I had no broken bones, no other injury. Everybody there looked at me as though I was from a different planet. It was a miracle. What is a miracle if it is not an intervention that comes from beyond? I believe an intervention came from the supreme God. I survived that accident with almost no physical damage even though the car's tire stopped on my body. If the lady had not stopped right at that instant, it might have been another story. It was a scary situation. I believe that my faith saved me that day.

The fact is many of you may have gone through such extraordinary circumstances. You may have witnessed or experienced near-death situations. Nothing could have justified the miss; there exists a natural force which is beyond our understanding that plays in the background of our lives. When we align ourselves with the vibration of that force, we become part of the force which transcends the mundane. Our lives transform and we radiate whenever and wherever we are. It is in connecting with that natural force that we are made complete and fulfilled. There is no one way to connect with that force. You could call it God, Universe, Cosmos, Infinite Intelligence, it doesn't matter. While some people in Africa and in other parts of the world believe in different gods, others such as the Christians, Buddhists, and the Muslims believe in approaching one God through different paths. Even Christianity has a variety of branches: Catholicism, Protestantism, the Jehovah's Witnesses and many other denominations. Some people engage in practices that give them a glimpse into a nonphysical world. In all, there is that sense of fulfillment or enlightenment that is the origin of spirituality. Spirituality is the final piece of the puzzle. No other achievement provides as much satisfaction and fulfillment as the lift of spirituality.

Some studies have revealed that those who believe are happier and more fulfilled than those who are not inclined to any form of spiritual practice. In principle, the believer who faces challenges will believe that God or whatever he believes in will come to his/her aid. They are not alone. They confide their challenges to their God or the Universe. Therefore, they are less prone to stress and worry. At the other end of the spectrum, a non-believer will wallow in despair if there is nothing he can do about a difficult situation. My being here in the United States of America is testimony to the power of God. Given the way I grew up, the conditions and situations of my family, it would have been absolutely impossible to even dream of coming to America; living day by day and lacking even the basic necessities of life doesn't provide much likelihood of a promising future. But I am here and the possibilities ahead of me seem endless. This part of self which is spiritual is the most fundamental part of our lives. When we don't have the connection with that part of self, life seems empty and meaningless. I have been fortunate to read biographies and come in contact with individuals deemed successful in their own right. What struck me was the source of their success; almost all tend to agree that spirituality plays an important role if not the *most* important role in success. They didn't say that their particular religion or practice was at the foundation. Most people agree there are different ways to elevate one's level of faith or spiritual state of mind.

Some people meditate by quieting their mind to transcend to this place where the mind and body become one. They often come out of it fuller, richer and renewed.

Other people pray for God to give them strength, peace, Love or whatever they lack.

In the end, it is all about attaining the level of greatness you are destined to reach.

Understanding Prayer

For our belief to become effective, it is not enough to think that we have faith and to leave it at that. That approach is usually the case when we grow up in a family with a certain religious belief or practice. We tend to identify ourselves with that religion even if we don't practice it. When we pray, we sometimes simply recite a memorized prayer, letting the words flow out. We often recite it out of ignorance to satisfy ourselves or to impress someone else. I believe that a moment of prayer should be a moment of utmost sincerity and complete devotion, a moment when nothing on the outside matters and no inner conversations are welcomed. Prayer should be a moment of presence and of the now. We should approach the moment leaving all baggage behind. Your heart and soul must be in harmony with what is being asked. The words or intentions that we speak must be emotionalized. At this stage the universe moves everything to provide the object of our desire.

Find a quiet place where you can concentrate; unclutter your mind and have a conversation with your God.

Chapter 8

Attitude is Everything

"What is the difference between an obstacle and an opportunity? Our attitude toward it. Every opportunity has a difficulty, and every difficulty has an opportunity."
— *J. Sidlow Baxter*

Our disposition toward others and the way we understand and approach the world is critical to our living a successful and fulfilling life; our best life ever. A positive mental attitude will in effect be the code that overrides any situation we encounter along life's journey. That code will help us rise above the mundane. A school of thought believes that attitude is genetic, that we are born with certain mental predispositions that allow us to carry ourselves through life. Others argue that it is the result of a conscientious decision to develop. No matter how our attitude comes to be, we possess the natural ability to influence it in order to attain our desired outcome. Therefore, one sure thing is that our attitude is what we make it. Our attitude is not defined by depending on situations and circumstances. It is our response to situations and circumstances that makes the difference.

Be Positive.

You may have been advised to be positive when you were going through challenging times. Being positive includes the comforting things people say to each other. We are often encouraged to look at the bright side of things. "Being positive" means seeing the glass as half full rather than half empty. What does this saying really mean? With a glass filled to the middle, one person will look at the glass and think the glass is half empty and another person will see the glass as being half full. Both people are correct. But the difference is the effect that each perspective has on oneself.

While thinking that the glass is half empty can motivate you to fill up the glass, this view primarily is a pessimistic view that promotes negative feelings. The view can lead to discouragement especially if we think that we have done so much already and perhaps have given all we can under the circumstances. Disappointment will follow and frustration will take over. At this moment, failure will be evident.

Looking at the glass as half full provides us with a positive feeling. It gives us a sense of accomplishment about how far we have come and about how much we have achieved. When we arrive at the level where we believe that the glass is half full, it is understood as the level of success we have achieved; it gives us an incentive to do more of what we have done already. Success usually comes in small incremental pieces accomplished every day. It is when we succeed at one level that we want to go to the next. Some people wonder why millionaires or billionaires want to make even more money and consider that desire to be greed. Others tell themselves that if they had a certain amount of money, they would stop working because they would be set for life. *Perhaps that is why the good Lord sees that they don't have that money.* It doesn't work that way. Success builds momentum. It provides the motivation to do more and accomplish more. It becomes a habit. People like Bill Gates, Warren Buffet, and Carlos Slim are, according to the recent Forbes list, the richest people in the world. They could stop striving and still be set for life along with their future generations. But they still wake up every morning, earlier than others, to go about the business of accomplishing more successes.

But the true test of being positive comes when the going is tough and the future looks dismal.

How can you be positive when you are hungry? This is the situation in which I lived for a most of the first two decades of my life, and there are millions of other people around the world who are facing that same situation now and don't have hope of the situation getting better. The question of being positive would sound impossible to them now.

How can you be positive when you or any one close to you is dying from an incurable disease? When hope doesn't seem to be a sentiment possible to be felt?

Or how can you be positive when you work hard day in and day out just to find out at the end of the month that you have fallen behind on your rent and other bills and you cannot put food on the table for your family. Worse yet, perhaps you lost your job and are not able to find another one. This happened to millions of American during the recent recession. They lost their jobs and have gone more than a year with no promise of a better situation.

All these scenarios are sufficient to cause the average person to fall prey to negative feelings and to perhaps feel absolute despair. Unfortunately, the majority of people find themselves crippled by these life situations.

But the answer to these questions should be, "Why not?" Why not be positive no matter what happens? Why not cultivate being positive? The idea is to gauge what serves you well. What will a negative attitude do to you and for you? I doubt it will solve a problem. I have yet to find proof that being pessimistic in face of adversities will alleviate the situation. On the contrary, many findings show that cultivating a positive attitude helps us overcome obstacles and maintain physical and emotional well-being.

As human beings, we possess different emotions that surface when triggered by interior or exterior factors. What makes the difference is our response to those stimuli. Between what happens to us and our response, there is a gap, according to Dr. Stephen Covey. It is what happens during that gap that determines the nature of our response.

Let's suppose that a stranger approaches you in the store and tells you that you are a bad parent because your child is crying hysterically and you can't seem to calm her down. Now, the incessant cry of a child may have already put a dent in your mood and this stranger pours salt on the wound. At this point you have two choices. Perhaps you recognize that this stranger has a problem of his own which has been brewing and the cry of the child was a trigger. (Then you completely ignore him and take care of your child and do your chores.)

Or you might think that this person is a shrink, and you wonder how he could have read you so well and accurately? (Then, you engage in the long tirade with him or her.)

Also, you might not have made peace with your spouse after a fight or a tense argument. In the morning you receive even more stingers from him or her just as you leave for a day's work. The same choice could apply here. You can choose to shrug it off or you can let it seep into the depth of your mind and soul. You can let that negative feeling follow you everywhere and ruin your day, making you cold and bitter toward coworkers and clients, turning the day into a disaster. The question is: is it worth being angry? The obvious answer to that question is, "No." I find it to be sad when I see people take pleasure in manifesting anger, resentment and grudges against others. I have friends and clients who often tell me how mad they are, how they are holding grudges against someone who has willingly or unwillingly done them wrong. But they don't understand that the problem is theirs and not that of the person they are angry at or holding a grudge against. While you have these negative emotions brooding inside of you, the intended person may not even be aware of your feelings and therefore sleep peacefully. You, on the other hand, are spending sleepless nights thinking about how you are going to avoid them or get back at them. It is clear that you are the one with a problem; you are the one suffering.

One day, a friend was giving me a ride to the mechanic so that I could pick up my car. He took a long city street to avoid traffic on the freeway. We were going toward the valley just before Wilshire Blvd. on Robertson when a white van made a slight cut in front of us. I saw it as no-big deal, but my friend became extremely irritated about the situation. He started to tail the van and during the process, dangerously cut off other cars. I tried to talk him out of that outrageous behavior. But he proceeded to drive alongside the other car and lower the passenger window to engage in verbal insults, gesturing fingers to the driver of the van. I was between him and the other driver. I was in the crossfire of verbal barrages and other exchanges. I have never been so scared because the other driver's face told me that the situation might fly out of control. I tried my best to neutralize the situation by telling a fabricated story that my friend's girlfriend just left him for a guy driving a white van. I was ready to tell my friend to drop me off then and there when the other guy appeared to understand what I said, and he rolled his window up. Even at that point my friend cut right in front of him and slowed down. It was only then that the van made a right turn and disappeared. My friend threatened to make a U-turn and follow him, but I insisted we call the police instead. After given up the idea of a chase or calling the police, I rode the remaining distance in silence while he kept cursing the other driver. After we arrived, I thanked him for the ride and we separated and I didn't mention anything about what had just happened. I waited till the next time I saw him and I asked him the question, "Was it worth it?" I didn't preach a sermon about how wrong and dangerous and reckless it was to act the way he did, although I was tempted to preach to him about good manners. But his response to the question was all I needed to hear. He even mentioned that the guy could have pulled out a gun. My friend's behavior was outrageous.

I believe this question should apply to anyone who engages in road rage or to any other rage-filled situation. Is it worth it? In our case my friend didn't know that driver and had never seen him before and there is a good chance they would never meet again. So why go through headache, heartache and other painful moments to get back at somebody? Shrug it off!

Being positive doesn't happen naturally or spontaneously. Maintaining a positive attitude requires a conscious, deliberate effort. It is a proactive decision. After all, it is a choice. It must become a habit in order to be effective. Just like any other habit, it must be cultivated day by day, moment by moment and situation by situation. So when you face a situation that requires your response, you have a chance to exercise that choice, that freedom.

There is a perfect way that I have cultivated over the years to become positive. That way is to find beauty in people or things and uncover the best in any situation, even in case of failure. Napoleon Hill puts it best when he says that every adversity and every failure brings with it the seed of an equal or greater benefit.

I recently participated in the Toastmasters International speaking contest. Winning the championship is like winning the American Idol contest minus the monetary prize. Your speaking career will take a giant leap. I was to represent my club at the area contest, the second level of the contest. I thoroughly prepared a speech. I had delivered that speech at my club and other clubs. I received evaluations concerning how I could improve and make the speech even more powerful. The evaluation part of a Toastmasters meeting is one of the most important parts. Because you cannot see yourself, other people can point out your flaws and qualities. During evaluation, you receive feedback by an assigned evaluator and other members regarding areas where you should improve, and you receive encouragement on things you do well. Evaluations had helped me tremendously to shape my speaking skills.

I worked and reworked my speech, and every time I delivered it, it became more powerful. It built in me confidence and assurance. I felt that speech would take me to the championship final. Everyone who listened to it thought it was a winning speech. The day of the contest arrived and I dressed professionally. When the Toastmaster of the contest introduced me as the first speaker, I told myself that the audience was about to take the journey of a lifetime. I took the stage and went on to do what I had prepared for. I walked the stage, looked people in the eyes and delivered punch lines. My voice took on a melodious tone, rising and falling when need be. Somebody told me afterward that the performance was like a symphony concert and that I was the conductor of the orchestra. After all the speakers had delivered their speeches, I felt that that was too easy and even members of my club and other clubs felt the same. Now, came the moment of truth: time for the result. When I heard a different name called for second position, my body relaxed, and my heart resumed its normal rhythm as the contestant who could have come in first came in second. I knew and everybody knew. I was almost on my feet to run up on the stage and get the trophy, ignoring even the surprised look on the face of the

Toastmaster who had seen the result already and expressed that there was a surprise. I ignored everything that could have given me a clue until he read the name of the winner. I felt as if I was knocked over by a sledge hammer or as if a Boeing 747 landed on my head. I sat down and seemed to disappear into the fabric of my chair. I tried to avoid people's gazes. What happened that day was anyone's guess. I felt ashamed.

A group of people wanted to know why I didn't win. They wondered if I had been disqualified for some reason. Their shock gave me a moment of relief.

I didn't just say, "Well I didn't win. Let's think positive." It didn't work that way. When you go through a major blow like that one, be aware of its effect on you; be in charge of the situation. That day, I knew I failed and I didn't suppress it, but I willingly let the effect brood inside me for the rest of the day. I talked to a few people about the event including my oldest daughter who was eleven years of age. It made me feel good .Out of that psychological gyration came a strong feeling of determination to become one of the best speakers the world has ever known. Some other logic came in mind about how winning could have jeopardized other plans down the road. And I became grateful I didn't win.

Cultivating a positive attitude requires trying to make the best of every situation or circumstance. For example, if you get fired from your job, you might look at it as an opportunity to finally work on that passion you have been nursing for a very long time. I started giving more focus to my passion when I quit my job for family health reasons.

You might lose a relationship to which you gave your

all. You might feel disrespected and betrayed. If you think hard enough, you will realize that relationship wasn't making you a better person, and that you ought to grow. Perhaps that relationship was not meant to be. Just think of anything positive that will make you feel better and more motivated. By now we know that the best revenge is massive success. You may be motivated to show the person who betrayed your love, your trust, your friendship that they have made a monumental mistake. This could be referenced with what Napoleon Hill in *Think and Grow Rich* called the, "transmutation of sex." Many of us might have already used this angle of motivation to accomplish great things in life. I certainly remember having done very well in grade school simply because I wanted to impress a girl in class. The point to be made is to use the experience to motivate you toward greater accomplishments.

Hell is Not the Others, be Good to People, Love people

I find it ironic when I hear people complain about others. You often hear them say they hate locations like DMV (Department of Motor and Vehicles) because it is overcrowded, how they loath cities like Los Angeles because it teams with people, how there are lots of nut cases out there. They seem to be genuine in their resentment toward others. This sentiment results from a self-centered attitude. Think of it this way. Hating other people for any reason simply implies that others have a right to hate you as well. That kind of thinking is a source of many problems in the society. When we begin to resent other people, we thereby resent our own nature since we are gregarious beings; consequently, we deny our own selves.

Human beings by nature are supposed to harmoniously live together and support each other. It is in the pursuit of the egoistic self-interest that we become wolves. This reality is well illustrated in all relationships. It is usually when one puts their own interests ahead of others that the bond breaks, whether it is a relationship of friendship, or romance or family. Deep down in the human soul exists the germ of togetherness that often surfaces during moments of calamity and disaster. People seem to bond for the greater good. When September 11th happened, I had newly arrived in the United States. I observed how in every corner of the country, people from different backgrounds and from all walks of life were united to stand strong in the face of the tragedy. So it wasn't only New York City that was touched by calamity; I too was pulled into this moment of national grief. That experience evidenced the power of oneness in humankind. This power is manifested all the time. As humans, we share a common humanity. We are human only in relation to other humans. Our humanity is bound up in one another. When a part of this connection is broken, if affects the whole. We all constitute the social fabric of this interconnected web.

In our own interest we are called to live together and support each other.

Jean Paul Sartre in his book **Hell is the Others** says that the devil resides only in other people and that others are the root of all evil, that it is in dealing with others that all hell breaks loose. Unfortunately, many people in our society today seem to profess that philosophy. But what we fail to see is that others are the mirror of what we are. It is true we can find the worst in human kind; so can we find the best? Whatever we seek in mankind we will find it. One's success can only come as a result of the success of others. In fact, if you give to people what they need, you will finally have what you want. The love of one another can open many windows of opportunity to become a better person. St. Francis of Augustine puts it best saying that it is in giving that we receive, in pardoning that we are pardoned so much to understand as to be understood, to console as to be consoled. And this is a golden rule in human relations, "Love one another." This is part of two summarized commandments taught by Jesus Christ two thousand years ago.

Love for one another glues us together and sustains our society. And it doesn't stop there. The principle must be applied to our day-to-day lives. You have to cultivate love and put people first before anything else you want to pursue. Many successful people believe that no matter what the calling, you will succeed only if you find a way to be of service. Otherwise, your chance of failure is great. We all know that no one can be an island. It is hard, almost impossible to accomplish anything without the help and support of other people. Others should be at the center of our lives and others should be a source of our motivation.

I didn't grow up as a gregarious person; I was not only shy, but I was afraid and insecure around people. As I learned to overcome this condition, I realized that being among others seems to heal and energize me. When I was working full time, I usually had to start at 5 AM. There were some nights that I could not get enough sleep. With little children, there is not always the guarantee of a full night sleep. I am not a coffee drinker, but I always discovered a rush of energy that would make me work until the end of my shift. It turned out that the source of my energy was people.

The fact is I like people. I like being around them. I like helping them. It is fascinating to understand what naturally motivates people to do what they do. I personally think that there is magic in loving. It has the power to transform lives and change the course of history. But you must allow it to happen and to benefit from it.

The secret of love of others resides in studying human beings and understanding them. In order to understand a person, we must listen to them. When we really listen to a person, we are giving to that person what Stephen R. Covey called the psychological air also known as empathic listening. Listening is one of the most important communication skills. When you listen, the other person opens up to you, confides in you and trusts you, and it is then that you can better understand that person. This approach helps avoid misunderstanding and misjudgment.

Imagine that you are working in customer service and somebody approaches you with a bad attitude and you respond in kind only to find out later that the person was confused because she had just gotten diagnosed with an incurable disease. How bad would that make you feel?

You have to understand that most of the time, hurtful or aggressive behavior is not intended to harm you personally. The perpetrator does not harbor resentment against you personally. You just happen to be the person they encounter. For example, some people take it personally when a car cuts in front of them in traffic. But it is important to take into consideration that the person might be in a hurry because he or she is late for a tyrannical boss. There could be children wailing in the back seat. The driver could be in a life or death situation. It is important not to make errors in judgment that strain relationships. When we show more interest in proactively listening, people connect with us in a deeper way. Our ability to listen to others will always lead to a more successful relationship with family, friends and colleagues. It is also a major factor in business, for example, in sales or any other level of business that requires human interaction.

Developing good relationships and getting along is beneficial to our social and emotional well-being because no one is an island, and our success often depends upon the success of others. The pursuit of our dreams must not be to the detriment of others, but rather it should serve others. There is a mutual benefit in being of service of others. Most of the time, having others as the end and not merely a means to an end is a noble goal that will bring rewards.

History provides us with a host of examples of those who put money first and manipulate people to attain that objective. Those individuals usually end up being exposed and going bankrupt. From an emotional well-being standpoint, it is from others we get comfort and healing.

I met a lady who told me that she was a member of Alcoholics Anonymous. She said that she had been sober for the past three months as of the writing of this chapter. I knew few details about the Alcoholics Anonymous program. She told me that she was alcoholic to the point of death. What really was helping her was being among others who had the problem and were willing to share their experiences. She said that the moments of sharing are the key that unlocks the awareness of the situation and the full comprehension of the danger it entails. It is usually when you see someone else going through the same struggle that you better understand your situation and take the first step to the cure. That young lady now takes enjoyment from being among people, not only friends from Alcoholics Anonymous, but also from other groups such as church groups where she can grow and contribute to a good cause. She finds in those groups the strength to stay sober, and eventually she gives advice to others about the danger of substance abuse. I believe she has the potential to do more than that with her story. Curiously when we first met, I was writing this chapter on the importance of being good to others, and that was why we hit it off right away. It seemed we were on the same wavelength.

Although we may find in our society some people who thrive only on despising others, we are by our nature "social animals," according to the Italian philosopher Spinoza.

We can only define our own existence in relation to the existence of others; sometimes our successes or failures can only have significance in relation to others.

Chapter 9

Be Motivated

"Of course motivation is not permanent. But then, neither is bathing; but it is something you should do on a regular basis."
— *Zig Ziglar,* Raising Positive Kids in the Negative world

To rise above the mundane to live an extraordinary life, you must keep the switch of motivation turned on. Motivation is the fuel of all action. It is the first step that engages the realization of our desires. One needs motivation to shed a few pounds in order to develop a nicely toned body. We need to be motivated to continue our education, to learn new skills, to work on our dreams. In brief, we need motivation to be and stay motivated. Otherwise, we will lose sight of the goal, of the objective, of our main focus. Motivation arouses us to take action which builds momentum and keeps us motivated.

Naturally, we are motivated by two things to accomplish whatever we seek: we want to either avoid pain or to experience pleasure. And our success in life depends either on the degree of pain we suffer or our success derives from the level of pleasure we enjoy. So our actions or lack of action are motivated by these two things. When we are aware of this playing field, we can consciously do the things that will satisfy our need. You may have heard stories of people who have risen from the depth of adversity and overcome great challenges to become successful, important people in the world. The examples of these people can be found in sports, entertainment, and politics and in other humanitarian enterprises. Each of us can list a few names. So many people who have attained the heights of glory are motivated by pain. They have worked hard to change their situations and better their conditions. And their life stories inspire us to do something positive with our own lives or at least they make us believe that it is possible. Believing that it is possible has been part of my transformation process. When we learn that another individual has achieved outstanding results by overcoming challenging obstacles, the knowledge gives us the incentive to believe that we can do the same. And sometimes the challenges they have overcome are far more difficult than our own. Then it seems possible for us.

In 2008 when Barack Obama became president of the United States of America, the belief system among minorities completely changed. African Americans have witnessed the dream of Martin Luther King, Jr. become a reality. It has given hope to the majority that the reality is possible for them. It is possible to pursue a dream, to become somebody, to choose one's own destiny.

In 2013, a 62- year-old woman, Diana Nyad completed the 110-mile-swim from Cuba to Florida. Her accomplishing such an objective at her age illustrates the outstanding power of the human spirit to achieve through determination. Her accomplishment constitutes a great motivation not only for those in her age category, but for all ages across the spectrum. We can all do what we set our mind to do. Her feat has certainly given me something to work on.

My Inspirations

When the idea of public speaking initially crossed my mind, I had a serious inner conversation. I came up with a series of facts that could have easily derailed me. I reasoned that English was not my first language; I could spend a lifetime just learning the language. I thought my accent was so thick that people would have a hard time understanding me. That fear was substantiated by the fact that I used to get laughed at by coworkers because they couldn't understand what I was saying. More polite people would ask me to repeat what I had just said.

I didn't know anyone who was a speaker at that time. I also thought that it required a full range of general knowledge. I thought I didn't have enough credentials. I didn't think I had what it took to become a speaker. These were the things some of my friends were telling me. Literally, I was facing dream killers on two fronts: the negative self-talk and the naysayers. I was beginning to surrender to these overwhelming factors until out of simple curiosity, I searched for an African speaker. I narrowed my Google search to *African who spoke French, but have become motivational speaker (maybe in the English language)*. I was trying to find somebody whom I could relate to and use as a model. Perhaps I could follow his or her path. I was not even sure if an English speaking African could help. Nevertheless, I came across one name that gave me hope and the motivation to pursue my dreams.

Rene Godefroy is his name and he is from Haiti. Even though he is not from Africa, I knew that English was not a language spoken in Haiti. So that would do. Then I learned more about him and found out that his upbringing was similar to mine. He grew up in a village while his mom was living in the city in Port-au-Prince. I grew up with my grandmother and my parents were living in the city of Douala. He suffered a great deal of hardship, too. When he came here to the United States, he washed cars and worked as a bellhop in a hotel. He went on to become a successful speaker doing an extraordinary job impacting lives in America and Haiti by creating a foundation to help the country that witnessed its share of natural tragedy in 2010.

When I looked at his background, I felt that we had lived similar lives in separate places and times; we both experienced abject poverty, the struggle for identity, difficulty in learning a new language and adapting to a new country. We traveled similar paths in our life's journey. "We are similar," I said out loud as though I was talking to somebody next to me. I formulated the conclusion that if this guy can achieve his dream, so can I. The fire of desire grew inside of me.

From that point on I renewed my desire to pursue this noble ambition to help other people by empowering and inspiring them to change and live their best life possible.

His advice through his videos and posts guided me to craft my own plan of action.

The journey of others, their lives and their stories can be a great motivation for our own lives. But we can't stop there. We constantly have to look for other reasons that push us to do what we have to do. Each individual can draw motivation from any number of sources. People will do extraordinary things because of others. It is often more rewarding than self-interest. The force of motivation seems to be stronger in that regard. Les Brown, one of the most renowned motivational speakers in the world often says that his motivation was to buy his mother a house. Others will want to succeed for their children. Even others will want to achieve greatness merely to prove that they can; the best revenge is massive success. You want to prove people were wrong when they said you can't do it. You want to succeed despite those who belittle you, who ridicule you about your ideas, who say that you don't have what it takes to do what you dream about. You get charged up, pumped up to prove that they are wrong.

What is Your Why for Your One Thing?

You have to find your *why*. It is the reason you take action to walk a specific path, to take that journey, to work on your dreams. If your *why* is strong enough, you can accomplish almost anything; you can do one more push up; run one more mile; read one more book; take one more class; take more training, learn one more skill; burn the midnight oil, get up the eighth time after falling seven times; forgive one more time; hang in there a little bit longer, go the extra mile. Sure you can.

You have to find the reason you should wake up early and go to bed late. What would make you keep going even if there were not much gas left in the tank? What would make you lift your head up, pump your chest high and make a fist? Without such reasons, you will give up at the first sign of failure; you will turn back and return to what is safe and comfortable. You will remain in the mundane.

It is important to consider the philosophy of an ant in order to rise up and live your best life. When a colony of ants starts on a journey, it will not stop in the face of any obstacle. It will go around it, above it or below it until it reaches its destination.

When you have defined the one thing that you believe is your purpose, you should devote every ounce of your being to its realization.

Some people make the mistake of thinking that it is important to have a Plan B in life. That simply means that if Plan A doesn't work out, you can still fall back on Plan B. This strategy is fatal for your dream. By forming a Plan B, you are planting in your subconscious mind the thought that you have another option and therefore you will never give your all to Plan A. You will likely abandon it after the first few failures. What if Abraham Lincoln gave up after he lost elections for the seventh time?

J. K. Rowling would not have become super successful today if she had had a Plan B. She would not have waited for *Harry Potter and the Sorcerer's Stone* to be rejected over twelve times before falling back on her Plan B.

Colonel Sanders received 1009 "nos" before he sold his famous recipe that became Kentucky Fried Chicken (KFC).

These are a few examples of those who have defined their one thing. They have persisted even after failures and rejections. Simply, they didn't have a Plan B.

I am not implying that once you determine your one thing you should quit your job to work on your one thing. It takes a good deal of time to realize a dream. You should make sure that your basic necessities are covered so you have the freedom to work on your goals and dreams.

People fall back on Plan B because Plan A is not really their one thing and their *why* is not strong enough.

These people are prone to turn to what is comfortable, to turn to what seems secure and tangible. Any idea that can possibly take them out of this zone will be deemed too risky and uncertain. Finding something to fall back on will be their safety valve.

I am lucky enough to have discovered that my one thing in life is being a speaker. Even though it is not the easiest thing to accomplish —nothing is easy about accomplishing a dream. I have to stay true and faithful to it. I had to find my *why* so I didn't give up in face of the obstacles. Already, I have faced discouragement and a ton of critiques from family and friends who find my decision ludicrous and delusional. Some of them believe that it is inappropriate to pursue such an idea when I am struggling financially. Others, without being open to me about it, secretly talked behind my back and looked at me as though I'd lost my mind. And sincerely, I don't blame them for trying to talk me out of accomplishing my desire. I might have done the same to others had I not worked hard to undo the negative thinking and beliefs that prevail in our communities.

If you are lucky to be surrounded by friends and family who encourage you, believe in you and even help you to accomplish your goals, it is important that you value them.

That could constitute your *why*. If not, you have to continue to find other sources of motivation.

But the idea is to keep the fire burning. We should feed our passion with a moderate dose of motivational intake, the same way we feed ourselves with nutritious food every day. Sometimes we may just need to hear from somebody else what we already know. It strengthens the belief. It is as simple as getting a second opinion. It reinforces what we know or believe for ourselves. Its objective is not to change our mind about the ideas we have, but the second opinion rather gives us validation and encouragement to go forward with our plans.

My motivation has always been provided by my extended family. From a very young age, I have prayed to be the shining star of my family, to be their hope, their bridge. I wanted to be the strongest link, to break the cycle of generational poverty in my family. To this day, when I think about my family, especially the ones that I left back home, I feel energized and determined. I know they sometimes lack food. After remembering that, I drop any unimportant pastimes to work on something that leads me toward my dream. For example, I will get busy writing, researching, reading, exercising or doing anything that will contribute to my success. Those thoughts always push me because I feel obligated to elevate my family so that food is no longer an issue. I am the only one given the opportunity to come to America, and I feel that it is my responsibility to do my part to make the family's wishes become reality.

To go about the task of pursuing your dream, to become a better person and be successful, you have to define your *why*. You have to keep your motivations alive.

This means that while you may have discovered the main reason why you want to accomplish your goals, you still have to find other sources of motivation to keep going.

When you are suffering in your relationships or financially or in another type of situation, the reality is the cavalry will not come to the rescue. You are on your own. What will keep you on your feet will be your decision to stand tall. Remember the prospect of sunshine following the rain. I believe that we need to remain motivated at all times in our lives, and many people don't seem to be aware of that reality. That is simply why many fail to stay on course and to pursue their dreams, to take care of the body, mind and soul and thereby focus of what matters in life.

We seem to be motivated by the things that are urgent rather than the things that are important. Many consider, for example, their health as important but do not classify it as the number one priority. But if a doctor were to prescribe an exercise regimen and good nutrition, I believe they would be obliged to comply. I sometimes employ the principle of negative motivation to push some of my clients to become more engaged in the issue that they are working on. I tell them to imagine, for instance, what it would be like if they could not work to provide for their kids because of becoming sick with an illness that could have been prevented by exercise and good nutrition. Or I tell them point blank to imagine having a heart attack or a stroke because the lack of exercise can lead to that consequence. This approach seems to work most of the time. It would certainly wake me up. But this type of motivation is not to be confused with the fear of illness. Whether or not we are parents, we should consider the possible consequences.

Maintaining good health will eventually impact the health of the family.

What will keep us going in the face of adversity, setback and failure is the ability to keep the fire burning. We must keep renewing the reason *why* we should continue, the reason *why* we should not stop.

Even though my family is my motivation to become better and achieve success, I must still look for small sources of motivation to help me through my days and weeks. Because every day that arises comes with a set of challenges I must overcome to keep afloat. It is about finding energy that sustains us during the day, finding a source of inspiration that keeps our minds focused on even the smallest thing that constitutes a step toward the goal we set for ourselves.

Some people pray or meditate first thing in the morning. This practice helps determine the day's outcome. No matter what happens during the course of a day, it will be determined in the realm of their mental and spiritual condition. Others will exercise to get the boost of energy to help them do their daily activities without interruption or compromise. Other people will think of someone they look forward to meeting or something that they look forward to doing. The anticipation provides a positive feeling that makes the day interesting. Scheduling a long due trip or vacation can also help motivate you to work harder and more efficiently since you will be getting away soon.

Another important source of motivation is achieving small successes. The technique of goal setting is how we measure success. Goal setting involves setting a goal that is time specific. For example, you could set a goal of losing 50 pounds in 6 months. You should not start exercising and then wait 6 months to see if you have lost 50 pounds. You must set mini goals. See the example below:

Goal	Target Time
Lose 50 lbs.	6 months
Lose 25 lbs.	3 months
Lose 8,5 lbs.	1month
Lose 2.2 lbs.	1 week

At the end of each week, if you have lost more than 2 pounds, you are making progress. That is a small success which will encourage you to continue what you are doing. If on the contrary you gain weight at the end of 1 week or 1 month, I doubt you will continue with your program. This strategy is true with any goal we set for ourselves. Success encourages more success. This principle, unfortunately, is used in casinos with slot machines that spit out wins during the first few rounds. We are programmed by nature to believe that the win will continue; unfortunately, it is rare that winning continues.

Chapter 10

Human Desires

"All bad behavior is really a request for love, attention, or validation"

—Kimberly Giles

Praise

As human beings, we yearn for praise and acceptance. William James the father of American psychology said, "The deepest desire in human nature is the craving to be appreciated." You can praise a child and watch him or her soar. This principle is also true for adults who seek to be appreciated. These notions have the power of motivation because to get a better outcome from someone, you need to validate them or praise them. In our society, when we observe people who carry out acts of violence and resent others, their histrionics could be caused simply because they lack validation or praise. They don't feel that they matter; their contribution doesn't count. They feel hopeless and careless. It is important that we give praise as often as possible. We will in turn be praised if only for our good sense of judgment and our ability to praise others.

When you validate or praise somebody, the receiver has incentive to live up to the praise and has the opportunity to prove that indeed he or she deserves praise.

One of my greatest assets is the power smile. Any encounter with another prompts a smile from me. It is an element that characterizes my personality. When I receive praise from people for the quality of my smile, I feel "forced" to smile even if I am having a very bad day. This "forced" smile will still lead me to get the effect of a returned smile. Science proves that even when you fake a smile, some activities in the brain release endorphins which are responsible for good mood. We can end up being happy even on the bad days. It is a win-win situation all the way around.

Feeling of Respect and Belonging

We all have a psychological need to be respected and to belong. These needs correspond to the third level of the classification of needs by Abraham Maslow that is called the Hierarchy of Needs. In the classification of needs, there are five levels of needs: physiological, safety, social, self-esteem and self-actualization. Maslow's philosophy stipulates that one must satisfy one level of need before going to the other level. When you are accepted in social groups, it is presupposed that you are on the third level of the hierarchy. It will therefore motivate you to go to the next level which is self-esteem. In general, even the simple, "Thank-you" when genuinely uttered has the potential to change the mood of our day.

Reward and Punishment System

A reward and punishment system is important to human achievement.

I had to leave work at the Trader Joe's company for family health reasons. During that time I didn't have a job. I took the opportunity to work on my dreams. I attended speaking and coaching workshops. I joined Toastmasters International to work on my speaking and leadership skills. I worked on anything that was related to my passion. Most importantly, I was working on myself. I achieved lots of personal growth. Because I couldn't yet earn a living from my dream, I had to return to Trader Joe's. Two months on the job, I got a promotion because I became even more valuable. With that promotion, I felt compelled to bring the best of myself to the company. Even if I had not been committed 100% to the company, that promotion would have changed my mind. I felt motivated to work hard and maintain commitment to the job.

A reward always reinforces the behavior that has led to it. We observe this process every day in children and in animals. Animal trainers use this technique to get animals to perform at the circus. With the reward system we feel motivated to repeat the behavior and possibly even do more than is expected of us.

Punishment can also motivate us to accomplish great things in our lives. I mentioned above that we do what we do either to avoid pain or to pursue pleasure. Punishment is a form of pain. We will do anything to avoid it. It is sometimes the source of justice, fairness and integrity. Avoiding pain and punishment leads to good results for ourselves and for others. We know that we may well go in prison if we steal. Unfortunately, many thieves steal anyway. The onus on drinking and driving can make us better people or it can prompt us to moderate our alcohol intake. The knowledge of the potential danger or pain can redirect our behavior toward something good. Society acknowledges that drinking and driving can lead to death.

In certain Toastmasters clubs, members have to give a penny every time they use filler words such as *eh, hum, so, but, like* and so on when speaking during a meeting. That practice motivates members to be aware of slips when they utter meaningless words or expressions. Avoiding those filler words makes a member a better speaker.

In my schools when I was growing up, there were varying degrees of punishment if you talked, ate or participated in a disturbance of any form. Those punishments included cleaning the classroom; sharing with everyone in class what you were eating; going to the teacher's home to perform work. Some students even received beatings on the buttocks or all over the body. The teacher was like a king in the classroom and students were usually quiet. I am not condoning these types of punishment, but they kept the students disciplined and respectful of authority and their elders. It certainly helped me in that regard.

There is another form of punishment that we can establish to control our own behavior. Some people use a rubber band on the wrist as a reminder of punishment of a particular behavior they want to stop. For example, they will snap it to their wrist anytime they curse or even start to have anxiety before an interview. The director of a certain company tried to cultivate a positive attitude in his company. He promised to give away $100 anytime he said something negative. The first day, he lost more than $2000; the next day he lost over $1000. By the end of the week, he was averaging saying one or two negative things, and eventually all employees followed suit. Small forms of punishment can be created to correct or avoid certain behaviors that stifle your progress.

Recently, a client that I was coaching told me he could not be consistent with the exercise regimen that we established for him. Since he lived in another state, I could not monitor him from afar to hold him accountable. I thought it would be too much to call him or send him a message to remind him about exercise; such a tactic doesn't really work. So together we figured a reward and punishment system that would work for him so that I didn't have to remind him. Because he liked to reward himself with a cocktail at the end of each day, he devised this punishment system. If he did not exercise, he would not get to have his cocktail. He called me a week later and told me that the day he was supposed to exercise was wearing on when he realized that it was almost time for his cocktail and he hadn't yet exercised. He quickly dropped down and did a series of exercises that took him about 15 minutes; then he had his cocktail which he savored with an air of pride. And he repeated the process until it became a habit.

The truth is he could have cheated; nobody was there to watch him or hold him accountable, but he made a commitment to himself and would have felt a great deal of guilt if he had a cocktail without exercising.

The system of reward and punishment can be applied to any situation we want to make better.

Chapter 11

Communication Skills for Life Transformation

"Take advantage of every opportunity to practice your communication skills so that when important occasions arise, you will have the gift, the style, the sharpness, the clarity, and the emotions to affect other people"

—Jim Rohn

The year that I was ten years of age and going into the equivalent of 6th grade, I was the most targeted subject of bullying in my school. Kids from my class and other classes were hammering me with insults whenever we crossed paths. They used to call me names and they even made up a song about me, not a good one. This particular day was a sport activities day. There was a soccer game between my school and another one. This kid cornered me by the mango tree where I was standing alone and told me that he was going to beat me that day. I hadn't done anything wrong; I was incapable of doing anything wrong unless it was by mistake. I was too afraid of attracting attention. He even offered me a choice as to where he would beat me. Either I must follow him behind the school or he was going to beat me in front of everybody.

I didn't want to be embarrassed in front of the other students. I followed him to the bushes behind the school and ended up falling into a hole left open by construction workers. I was buried to the neck. After he left, I managed to dig out of the ground, and I never spoke to anyone about the incident.

I grew up suffering from a sort of disease called an inferiority complex. I believed that everyone was better than me. I believed I was a nobody and amounted to nothing. Maybe it was because we lacked almost everything and often suffered from hunger. I thought for that reason I was inferior. That belief paralyzed my ability to express myself or to defend myself against attack. The boy in this case was smaller than me. All things considered, he was no match for a fight. But I was not able to even report the incident to the school staff. I became the student who never spoke in class unless called on by the teacher. Even then, my body would spasm; my voice would barely be audible even to the student sitting next to me. If I didn't understand something in class, I would never ask that it be repeated or clarified. I struggled because of the inability to speak up. I carried this malady into adulthood.

Today I can say with great confidence that the ability to communicate well is changing my life before my eyes. It has given me the tools to create a meaningful purpose for myself.

Communication is the means by which we interact as human beings. We learn to understand ourselves and others by communication. Most of the time, humans get into conflict because they misunderstand each other; there has been a gap in communication. Improving our communication skills will not only help avoid misunderstandings, but communication is the key to positively interacting and affecting people. Several components comprise effective communication skills.

Listening Skills

All good communication skills start with good listening skills. Listening skills are the most important aspect of communication and are fundamental to our effective interaction with others. Most of us fail to acquire listening skills, and the result is all manner of conflict, whether it is between individuals or nations. We don't take time to listen, to understand other people, to see what they see and feel what they feel. This lack of listening skills is even more pronounced when there is tension between two or more individuals. At this stage everyone will become firmly locked in their belief and reject anything that is not in alignment with their mindset. This position is well evidenced in couples' relationships where one does not listen to the other. Misunderstanding sets in.

But what is listening really?

Listening is the ability to open one's ears to someone who is talking. We often engage in different aspects of listening.

Sometimes, while a conversation is going on, a person's eyes can be fixed on the other person, but the person's mind is far away. We cannot respond in kind because we will miss the point of the conversation.

Sometimes, our attention fades in and out. We only pick up on some of the things being said. We often get distracted by things in our peripheral vision. This can also happen because we feel fatigued or when the conversation is boring.

There sometimes comes a moment during the conversation when we interject our own story into the conversation. This situation reminds me of an actor who memorizes the script and jumps in with his line without understanding what the other actor is saying. Imagine the other actor had made a mistake and said something unexpected. A disaster can ensue. We sometimes miscalculate and chime into the conversation telling the other person our own problems hoping to establish a bond and create sympathy. The desired effect may not occur because some people only want to be listened to. They don't want you to add to their pain. When they are already feeling the pain of their own problems, you could be adding your pain to theirs.

Sometimes we interrupt to offer our response without letting the speaker finish.

These examples do not illustrate good listening skills and they cause misunderstanding.

Effective listening skills involve physical and emotional presence. Presence simply means that we have to be present physically with the talker and according to Western culture, we must look into the eyes of the person who is talking. In other cultures, looking someone in the eyes is not a requirement of good listening skills. It might rather constitute a sign of disrespect. But let's stay in the Western context. Maintaining emotional presence is the most important aspect of listening skills because of the phenomenon of emotional osmosis marked by sympathy and empathy. The listener internalizes what is being said and feels what the talker is going through. The effect of this transfer of emotions is really what connects the two people. Rapport is built and a bond is established. We are in for a great conversation. To accomplish that, it is also necessary to pause for about 3 to 5 second after the person stops taking. The reason for the pause is to avoid interrupting. Perhaps the person is just catching his breath before continuing. Pausing will allow the talker's words to sink in and provide better understanding.

With regard to this definition of effective listening, we should listen more than we talk. The Greek philosopher Epictetus said, "We have two ears and one mouth so that we can listen twice as much as we speak." This message is as true today as it was thousands of years ago.

The art of communication begins with the art of listening.

The Power of Vocabulary

Many do not consider vocabulary as something that matters much in life. But the question that begs to be answered is, "What really matters in life?" Many would say that money and happiness matter most. What we fail to realize is that vocabulary is fundamental in getting us to the place in our lives where our vision of the world is expanded, and the new vision helps us formulate a definition of our own notion of happiness. Our ability to make money in our chosen career field can depend upon communicating well. The use of good vocabulary is of paramount importance.

Vocabulary is simply a tool that helps us interpret and understand the world. It is through that tool that we can translate what we see, hear and feel. When equipped with that tool, our vision of the world will be expanded and we will be able to create a reality in which we can see possibility, opportunity and happiness.

When it comes to expressing ourselves, we can only convey with clarity our inner feelings by using words that are appropriate and meaningful. I remember when my arsenal consisted of a handful of words in the English language. I struggled to understand people and to express myself. Everything seemed to escape me and I realized that indeed I was in a foreign land. Unfortunately, many of us who immigrated in the United States have to suffer from this integration process. But we don't have to remain stuck there. Learning any language is a never ending process. And this principle applies even to naturally born speakers of a language. It is estimated that the vocabulary in the English language, for example, is roughly more than a million words, but the most common words amount to three hundred.

So how many words are in your vocabulary?

A link connects vocabulary with behavior. A study of prisoners showed that among the inmates studied, the lower the level of vocabulary, the poorer the behavior. The inmates with a small vocabulary tended to be aggressive and were inclined to poor behavior. While the study was conducted on inmates, the issue of vocabulary applies to all humans. Conversely, you may have noticed that great communicators are also great leaders, and vocabulary is an important factor in developing great communication skills. You can see the transformation. There is no better way to increase your vocabulary than by voracious reading. Another effective way is to subscribe to *the word of the day* on the Internet. You will receive in your email inbox the *word of the day* every day and you can learn it and apply it in a sentence of your own. By taking action to increase your vocabulary, your vision of the world will completely be transformed.

Body Language

Body language is a set of signals the physical body conveys during an interaction. Body language is the most essential part of communication. It is also known as non-verbal cues. These non-verbal cues constitute about 80% of communication. It is the most important part of communication because it doesn't lie. It is the body's natural expression of what is happening on the inside. These movements are for the most part involuntary. Most of the time, we do not express our true feelings. There is a number of reasons. An example demonstrating the interpretation of body language was the Lewinsky scandal when experts analyzed the non-verbal cues in Bill Clinton's response to the sex allegations. Many of those experts concluded that although there was an emphatic denial by

Clinton, he indeed lied.

The non-verbal cues can range from arm-crossing to eye-rolling. Other signals include rapid blinking of the eyes, nose rubbing and, pointing toes toward the door. For example, when we observe someone with their head lowered and shoulders sagging, it is a sign that they lack confidence or that they are in a depressed mood. Also, when someone you are talking to folds their arms across their chest, you should reconsider what is being said as they are assuming a defensive position.

The importance of knowing non-verbal cues is to understand other people and act based on that understanding. Your ability to understand and read non-verbal cues will provide you with an unfair advantage in negotiation situations, in interviews and many other situations. Professional speakers use this concept to engage their audience.

Great communicators are masters of body language techniques.

Learning the Skill of Communication

I came to become a better communicator when compared to the introvert that I was growing up. I became aware of my situation and made a deliberate decision to learn how to communicate well. It was not long ago that I came to that conclusion. As part of my personal development, I joined the organization called Toastmasters International. It empowers its members to foster confidence by becoming better communicators and better leaders.

Toastmasters teaches every aspect of communication. The organization believes that as social and political animals, we have to always stay ready anywhere we go for any impromptu speaking opportunity that comes our way. During Toastmasters meetings, there is a practice that consists of asking a random question and calling on random members to answer, comment, or say something in a limited time. This is where the power of vocabulary is most important. Because there is not time to think and organize your thoughts, you will stutter if you don't have words ready. The more you engage in these extemporaneous talks, the better prepared you will become for participating in spontaneous street interviews and expressing viewpoints on different subject matter.

Body language is also something you learn to control during a speech at a Toastmasters meeting. In order for your message to make an impact, you have to be able to match your body movements with the idea you intend to convey. For instance, it will send mixed signals to tell a sad story and have a smiling expression, and vice versa.

Toastmasters' functionaries are assigned to cultivate listening. If you are assigned to evaluate a speech, you have to pay attention to the small details as you can't afford to be distracted. Not only are you required to watch every movement and expression of the speaker, but you also have to listen for the use of correct language, the structure, volume, grammar and the message in the speech.

That in a nutshell is how that organization has made me who I am today.

Communicating well is vital to improving one's confidence. My passion to help people with their lives has been solidified with the ability to communicate my message with clarity. Many friends who knew me growing up firmly believe that I am a different person now. The reason is simple; communication skills have changed me.

Communication is the skill to acquire. You don't have to be a speaker, a salesperson or someone in the field of journalism to be a better communicator. It is the skill of life. It is what lawyers need in courtrooms to plead their cases. You could have all the evidence and someone with great communication skills will easily shred your case with arguments. Communication is the key that harmonizes the family. When your teenage kid's entire vocabulary is limited to one- or two-word-responses to any question, it is time you became a better communicator. Better leaders are great communicators.

When you become a better communicator, your life is transformed, and you acquire a bigger vision for yourself.

www.ingramcontent.com/pod-product-compliance
Lightning Source LLC
LaVergne TN
LVHW011239080426
835509LV00005B/560